You're
the
Business

Anna Codrea-Rado is a journalist, podcaster
and campaigner.

Her writing appears in the *New York Times, Guardian,
Wired, Monocle* and many others. As a campaigner
for freelance workers' rights, she launched the
#FairPayForFreelancers campaign and the Freelancer Pay
Gap tracker. She's also the co-host of the number one
careers podcast, *Is This Working?*, alongside the writer
Tiffany Philippou.

In 2017, when she first went freelance, Anna started a
newsletter about her experience of losing a job and striking
out on her own. LANCE has since grown into a weekly
staple for tens of thousands of readers, who turn to it for its
candid advice on how to be happy and successful working
for themselves.

You're the Business is her first book.

)

HOW TO BUILD A SUCCESSFUL CAREER WHEN YOU STRIKE OUT ALONE

ANNA CODREA-RADO

For anyone who ever dreamed that maybe things could be better if they just lived life on their own terms

001

Ebury Edge, an imprint of Ebury Publishing,
20 Vauxhall Bridge Road,
London SW1V 2SA

Ebury Edge is part of the Penguin Random House group of companies
whose addresses can be found at global.penguinrandomhouse.com

Penguin
Random House
UK

First published in the United Kingdom by Ebury Edge in 2021

www.penguin.co.uk

A CIP catalogue record for this book is available from
the British Library

ISBN 9780753558652

Typeset in 11/16pt Sabon LT Std
by Integra Software Services Pvt. Ltd, Pondicherry

Printed and bound in Great Britain by Clays Ltd, Elcograf S.p.A.

The authorised representative in the EEA is Penguin Random House
Ireland, Morrison Chambers, 32 Nassau Street, Dublin D02 YH68.

Penguin Random House is committed to a sustainable future for
our business, our readers and our planet. This book is made from
Forest Stewardship Council® certified paper.

Contents

Part One:

Freelancing Fundamentals

CHAPTER ONE

Setting Up

On an unremarkable Friday afternoon in the summer of 2017, I lost my job.

I was called into a meeting room at work and my boss's boss Skyped me from the New York headquarters to let me know that I was being made redundant. The website I'd worked for as an editor for the previous two years was being shut down and nearly all its staff were being let go, effective immediately. In a state of shock, I packed up my desk, left the office in the middle of the afternoon and went home.

Over the weekend, my mum took me out for lunch to console me. She was telling me everything would be fine and that I'd find a new job soon when I heard the words come out of my mouth: 'I've already got another job. I'm freelance now.' Sure enough, when Monday morning rolled around, I got up and went into the kitchen where I sat at the table, opened up my laptop and started freelancing.

In the year before I lost my job, I'd already thought about going it alone. I would sit at my desk in the windowless basement at my staff job and daydream about what it would be like to make a living from my own home. Not having to deal with the politics of an office, or indeed the commute to it, sounded like my kind of career. It wasn't just my allergy to the office that made me suspect I was better suited for self-employment

– as someone who thrives on variety and who struggles with being told what to do within a rigid professional hierarchy, I've always felt hemmed in by any job title I've held.

But it took a redundancy to finally push me to make the leap. I'd been too scared to go freelance up until then because I'd heard the horror stories about how precarious self-employment was and I believed them. I was worried that I wouldn't be able to make the finances work, that I wouldn't find any clients, that I'd drown under a pile of crumpled receipts trying to file my own tax returns.

What I realise now is that I was telling myself freelancing wasn't viable because I refused to believe that it was possible to have my dream career come true. I was hiding behind excuses of a regular pay cheque, holiday and sick pay, and staying in a job that made me miserable. But when all the things I thought I had to lose were gone, I realised it was time to make a change. In spite of the circumstances that prompted the start of my freelancing, by the first anniversary of my redundancy I'd had the best year of my career. I was writing for publications I'd once only dreamed of, including a front-page story in the *New York Times*. I was earning more than I had done in my staff job. And, most importantly, I'd never felt more fulfilled in all of my working life.

The horror stories didn't materialise but I did have to adjust to freelance life, which opened my eyes to a completely different way of working than I was used to in traditional employment. When I started my very first job, I was shown around the office, my new colleagues took me for lunch and the HR worker handed me an employee handbook. None of that happened when I went freelance. No one showed me how to go about doing my work, no one invited me out for lunch and there was no handbook to reference. I was on my own.

Freelancing isn't 'better' than working in-house, nor is freelancing a solution to work-based problems. My own story isn't about quitting a job, going freelance and living happily ever after. It's about figuring out how to make working for myself work for the long haul, because I truly believe that it can be a viable career plan for those who choose to work differently. When I look back over the course of my freelancing career to date, there's so much I wish I'd known. I needed a resource to guide me through the ups and downs, a handbook I could keep on my desk and reference whenever something unexpected came up.

So, I wrote it all down. I wrote *You're the Business* to be your own personal freelance cheerleader. I've filled it with everything you need to know to work for yourself, including all the lessons I've learned and some inspiration from a few superstar freelancers. I hope this book can be something you turn to when you have a problem that needs solving, that it brings you comfort when times are hard and, ultimately, that it gives you a roadmap for happiness and success when you strike out alone.

In this chapter, you'll learn:

- What working for yourself means
- Your rights when you're a freelancer
- The difference between a sole trader and limited company

What Does Working for Yourself Actually Mean?

As I was about to start writing this book, I was procrastinating under the thinly veiled guise of spring cleaning my office. While sorting through an old box, I found a notebook I'd bought in 2016 when I was still in a staff role and plotting out my dream of self-employment. I opened the notebook and on the first page I'd written 'Why I want to go freelance' across the top. The first point I'd noted down was 'A greater sense of self-worth from doing something completely independently'. I'd also written that I wanted more autonomy over my time, greater flexibility in my career and to be proud of myself for trying new things.

Reading over that list, I was taken straight back to a time when I was unfulfilled in my professional life and imagining what working for myself might be like. I remembered writing it and a little voice in the back of my mind telling me that it couldn't possibly be as good as I was dreaming. And yet, on reflection, it has been.

Finding that list got me thinking about what we actually mean when we say we work for ourselves. For me, being freelance means a lot more than just an employment status. Working for myself means living life on my own terms – it's a life choice as much as it is a job. In working for myself, I've learned as much, if not more, about who I am as a person as I have about business. For instance, I've realised that I am enthused by helping other people solve a problem. I've also learned hard lessons, like how I tangle up what I do for work with too much of my identity. Knowing myself better – what motivates me and what I'm passionate about – has helped me create a more fulfilling career.

If you could design your day, your job, your career from scratch, what would it look like? And why? That 'why' is very important. Because in working for yourself you get to design every aspect of your career and the best way to do that is by starting with what compels you to do your work in the first place.

I've come to realise that I struggled to find professional fulfilment in in-house roles not because I was bad at my job but because the job was bad for me. I used to be frustrated in staff roles because I felt like I had no say over the decisions that affected my working life and yet I didn't want to move into the kind of position in which I would be able to influence them. As far as I was concerned, there was a management paradox. In order to accelerate in my career, I would need to assume managerial responsibilities. However, that path would only take me further away from writing, creating a gulf between me and the work I love. In working for myself, I've been able to design a career that stretches me while not compromising on the work itself. I've found a deep sense of self-worth from my work as a result.

That's not to say self-employment is without compromises; of course there are concessions. No sick pay, no annual leave and paltry parental allowance are structural issues that can make this a challenging career choice. Nonetheless, there are many myths about freelancing I don't find to be true. For instance, I take issue with the idea that freelancing is insecure work. Yes, it's insecure in the sense that there isn't a safety net like the one that catches in-house workers. But you can't get fired from freelancing. Your business can't get sold from under you and no one will restructure your team. There are new and different challenges you'll face when you work for yourself but, on a day-to-day basis, I find the agility of freelancing actually makes me more able to weather the storms.

Working for yourself means different things to different people. It can be a stepping-stone for some. For others, it's a side hustle. There are many – I count myself among them – who are in it for the long haul. Working for yourself can be a dream job, an illustrious career or simply a way to pay the bills. It can also be all three. Whatever it is, it's yours for the making.

The Different Ways to Work for Yourself

What's in a name?

When you work for yourself, the freedom of how to work extends to what you call yourself professionally.

There are now over 5 million self-employed workers in the UK, according to the latest figures from the Office of National Statistics. That's just over 15% of the country's workforce and it's a varied group that includes freelance graphic designers and writers, artists and florists, as well as IT consultants, virtual assistants and delivery workers.

Depending on the type of work you do, the industry you're in and your own personal preference, there are different titles you can give yourself. You can describe yourself either by how you do your work, by what the work is or by its legal classification. For example, I'm a freelancer, an author and a sole trader.

It's important to note that the UK's tax authority, HM Revenue and Customs (HMRC), only considers you to be 'self-employed' if you are a sole trader, meaning that you and your business are the same entity. If you own a limited company, you're not classed as self-employed by HMRC. Instead, you're both an owner and an employee of your company. (I'll go into the differences between sole traders and limited companies in more detail later on in this chapter.)

Of course, how you're registered with the tax authorities and how you talk about what you do don't have to be the same thing. Most people understand 'self-employed' to be a blanket term, applicable to anyone who works for themselves rather than receiving a wage or salary from an employer. And while there might be a technical term for what you do, you might prefer to call yourself something else. Except in conversations with my accountant, I never talk about myself as a sole trader. Instead, I interchangeably describe myself as either a freelancer, self-employed or a journalist.

It's like when you work in-house and your job title doesn't actually reflect what it is you do, so when you're at a networking event, you call yourself something else. I once worked at a university as a marketing executive, where my main job was to edit a magazine, so I'd tell people I was an editorial assistant. I did this because I was establishing my writing career and I wanted to signal to others – and to myself! – that I was on the right path.

Let's look at some of the different job titles you can give yourself:

Freelancer

In the UK, 'freelancer' is neither a legal term nor a tax status. It's really more of a cultural term for a type of worker. As such, each freelancer has their own definition of what they do, but generally speaking a freelancer will have multiple clients at the same time, do their work at home and set their own hours. The work is usually project-based and income is earned through either a project fee or a daily or an hourly rate. The creative industries tend to be those where the term freelancer is used the most. You'll generally hear about freelance writers, photographers, graphic designers, illustrators, hair stylists and makeup artists.

Independent worker

An independent worker does what it says on the tin – they work independently. It's a newer term that's recently come into the work lexicon. While it essentially means the same thing as freelancer, some people prefer to call themselves independent workers. Generally, people who work in more progressive sectors such as innovation, technology and research tend to call themselves independent workers.

Contractor

A contractor typically works on one project for a client at a time. Often, the fees for this work are paid at a daily or hourly rate. A contractor can be a sole trader, a limited company or employed by an agency or umbrella company. In industries like IT, construction and consulting it's more common to hear the term contractor than freelancer.

Small business owner

This might be someone who runs a florist shop and employs a part-time assistant, but it could also be someone who runs an online brand consultancy out of their kitchen. While small business owners are usually associated with products and/ or physical premises, plenty of self-employed workers like the title because it denotes a degree of professionalism. You also sometimes hear the term 'micro business owner'. Some people start out as freelancers and grow into small business owners, either in size or in mindset.

Entrepreneur

The term is now synonymous with Silicon Valley, however, an entrepreneur is really just anyone who sets up their own business. The term carries a certain cachet, of someone who's doing something innovative or disruptive, usually in the tech space. For that reason, most people who work for themselves in the tech industry call themselves entrepreneurs, while others avoid it because of its 'tech-bro' associations. The term 'solopreneur' has also started creeping into use, to describe people who innovate like an entrepreneur does, but work by themselves rather than as part of a team.

Gig worker

People who work in the gig economy are considered contractors; the difference is that rather than working on a project basis directly for a client, they work on demand, usually through a third-party platform. There's a lot of flexibility with this kind of work, especially in terms of hours, but securing it is dependent on the availability on the platform. Ride-sharing drivers, delivery people and skills-for-hire are the most common types of gig worker.

Side hustler

A side hustler is a part-time freelancer. They have a nine-to-five job and do their freelancing on the side.

What should I call myself?

I pay special attention to the words I use to describe my employment status. I hate it when I'm filling out a form and I come to the question where I'm asked to choose between 'full-time employed' and 'self-employed'. It's a subtle semantic difference that really gets under my skin because the implication is that if you work for yourself, you're not doing so on a full-time basis. Instead, as you'll see in this book, I distinguish between freelancers or the self-employed and their 'in-house' or 'staff' counterparts.

I call myself a freelancer because I like the original definition of the word. The term 'free lance' was coined by the Scottish writer Sir Walter Scott in his 1819 novel *Ivanhoe* to describe medieval mercenaries. 'I offered Richard the service of my Free Lances, and he refused them,' Sir Walter wrote. 'A man of action will always find employment.' These men offered their lancing skills to any wealthy landowner who would pay the best price for them.

I love the idea that working for yourself dates back so far, that charging your worth is, quite literally, mercenary. However, you might be thinking that you don't like the connotations of the word 'freelancer'. I've found that many people avoid the term because it sounds too casual and they want to establish themselves as a professional expert. And that's OK, you get to call yourself whatever you want (you may even prefer a term I've not listed here).

As you think about what to call yourself, take practical considerations into account – for example, how do other workers in your field and industry refer to themselves? But also think about your identity as a worker and as someone who's chosen to forge their own career path.

Know Your Rights

There's a common misapprehension that freelancers have no rights. While it's true that employment law doesn't cover self-employed people, there are nonetheless other laws and protections that apply to freelancers. For instance, as a self-employed person, you still have protection for your health and safety and, in some cases, protection against discrimination. If you do fall foul of illegal practices, you have the right to pursue damages, which I'll cover in later chapters.

While there might not be as many rights that protect the self-employed, that doesn't mean you can or should be taken for a ride by nefarious clients. It's vital to learn what rights you do have and to support those who campaign for more of them. When you don't know what your rights are, you leave the door open for clients to take advantage of you.

The way that I think about self-employed rights is that it's my responsibility to make sure I protect myself as best I can. If I worked at a company, there would be a health and safety officer there to make sure the staff are protected. I'm my own health and safety officer and it's my job to make sure I'm looked after.

Discrimination

It's against the law for employers to treat their workers unfairly or differently because of who they are and, in some cases, the legislation also applies to freelancers. The Equality Act 2010 makes it illegal to discriminate against anyone because of age, gender reassignment, marital status, being pregnant or on maternity leave, disability, race – including colour, nationality, ethnic or national origin – religion or belief, sex or sexual orientation. If you feel you've been the victim of discrimination while carrying out your work, Citizens Advice can help you.

Health and safety

The Health and Safety at Work Act lays out how employers must protect the health, safety and wellbeing of anyone on their premises, including any freelancers. Put simply, if you do any work on a client's premises, you're entitled to the same health and safety protections as the in-house staff.

Whether you have to comply with the law yourself depends on the work you do. If your work activity is specifically mentioned in the regulations set out in the Act – including work in construction, agriculture or railways or work with gas, asbestos or genetically modified organisms – then you have to undertake a risk assessment. Even if you don't work in those areas, you may still have to make sure you're compliant with the act if your work poses a risk to the health and safety of others. For example, the law would apply to a hairdresser who uses bleaching agents or similar chemicals but not to one who only washes and cuts hair.

The Health and Safety Executive is the body that enforces the law and you can find out if the work you do is covered by these rules at www.hse.gov.uk/self-employed

Late payments

An important law that all freelancers in the UK should be aware of is the Late Payment of Commercial Debts Act. This entitles you to claim interest and debt recovery costs if another business is late paying for goods or a service.

If you agree a payment date, the regulations recommend that it be within 30 days for public authorities or 60 days for private companies. If no payment date has been agreed, the law says the payment is late 30 days after either the customer gets the invoice or you deliver the goods or provide the service (if this is later).

If a client is late paying, you can claim interest, plus a fixed sum in late payment fees. The interest you can charge if a business is late paying you for goods or a service is known as 'statutory interest' and is 8% plus the Bank of England base rate for business-to-business transactions. You cannot claim statutory interest if it's different from the rate specified in the contract, so make sure you read your contracts carefully. If your contract is with a public authority, such as a local council or the NHS, you cannot use a lower interest rate either.

You're also able to claim an additional fixed sum on top of the interest, which is set by the legislation and depends on the amount of the debt. For debts up to £999.99, you can charge a late payment fee of £40, for amounts between £1,000 and £9,999.99 it's £70 and for anything over £10,000 it's £100. You can only charge the business once for each payment, however, you can charge a fee for each late invoice. So, if you've done three pieces of work for a client and issued three separate invoices for them, you can charge three late fees. There is more information on how to deal with late payments in chapter 11.

Maternity Allowance

The self-employed do not qualify for statutory maternity pay. Instead, you can claim Maternity Allowance. The amount you can get depends on your eligibility. You could get either £151.20 a week or 90% of your average weekly earnings (whichever is less) for 39 weeks, or £27 a week for either 14 or 39 weeks. To claim Maternity Allowance, go to www.gov.uk/maternity-allowance to access the forms. There's a guide to navigating parental leave for freelancers in chapter 10.

State pension

Self-employed people have a right to a state pension. You can only receive a state pension if you've paid the necessary national insurance contributions via HMRC. There's a guide to self-employed pensions in chapter 10.

Welfare benefits

Self-employed workers have the right to claim benefits. If you're on a low income or out of work, you may be able to claim Universal Credit, which is a monthly payment to help with your living costs. You can see if you're eligible at www. gov.uk/universal-credit/eligibility

Contracts

In the absence of robust employment law, the best way to protect yourself as a freelancer is through a contract. A contract outlines all the particulars of the relationship between you and your clients and what's expected of both parties, including timely payment. If your client doesn't offer you a contract, you can use a platform like Underpinned (www.underpinned.co) which offers a contract building service. You can also buy contract templates from online legal service providers like LawBite (www.lawbite.co.uk) or a solicitor's firm that specialises in legal matters for small businesses.

How to Set Up Your Freelance Business

As I mentioned at the start of this chapter, there are two different ways to structure your business when you work for yourself:

Sole trader

As a sole trader, you run your own business as an individual and are considered self-employed by HMRC. You can keep all your business's profits after you've paid tax on them. You and your business are the same entity so you're personally responsible for any losses your business makes.

Limited company

A limited company is a separate entity that you can form to run your business (even if that business is just you). A limited company is either 'limited by shares' or 'limited by guarantee'. Companies that make a profit are usually limited by shares and not-for-profits are limited by guarantee. In both cases, the company is legally separate from the people who run it and has separate finances from your personal ones.

Benefits of being a sole trader

Less paperwork

Setting up as a sole trader is straightforward. You just have to let HMRC know that you're going to be paying your tax through self-assessment, which can be easily done online (more on that later in this chapter). You also have less paperwork to file once you're up and running as you only need to submit an annual tax return, whereas a limited company director also needs to complete corporation tax returns and annual accounts.

Few admin costs

As the administrative responsibilities of being a sole trader are less burdensome, your bookkeeping is straightforward and as such you won't need to have an accountant. Even if you do choose to hire one (which many sole traders do), the fees for filing sole trader accounts are less expensive than for limited companies.

Privacy

Limited companies must register with Companies House (the UK's registrar of companies) and certain personal details will be made available online, including company details.

Benefits of being a limited company

Liability

The key difference between a limited company and a sole trader is that as a company, your business is a separate entity from you. This means that should something go wrong in your business, only your business is liable. For example, if you were sued for breach of contract, only your business assets (such as the money in your business bank account and any professional equipment you have) would be on the line, but your personal assets (such as a property or personal savings) are protected. Similarly, your personal assets can't be taken from you to pay for any business debts if you get into financial difficulty.

Profit potential

The way you pay tax as a limited company is different from that of a sole trader. Sole traders pay tax on all the profits they make after deducting business expenses. Limited company directors pay corporation tax and income tax on any dividends they take. At a certain profit level (usually £50,000), you may end up paying less in tax compared to the same earnings of a sole trader. (There is more on how tax works in chapter three.)

Credibility

Depending on the industry you work in, operating as a limited company can carry professional cachet. For example, in the IT industry, it's generally expected that self-employed contractors be registered as a limited company. It's also important to research this as some larger companies will only deal with freelancers whose businesses are structured in this way.

Borrowing power

As a limited company, you have more options for raising capital and borrowing money.

Which structure is right for me?

While there may be tax advantages with one structure compared to the other, there are also other factors to take into account, such as the nature of the work you do; your capacity to take on additional admin responsibilities; how other freelancers in your industry are structured; your clients' expectations; your long-term plans for your business and your personal circumstances outside of work.

Given the financial and legal implications, it's important to seek advice from an accountant or financial advisor about which option is best for your circumstances. This is true whether you're planning on freelancing for the long haul or are starting a side hustle. Remember, you can set up as a sole trader when you start out and then become a limited company as your business grows.

How to set up as a sole trader

When you register for self-assessment with HMRC, you are essentially telling the tax authority that you will be filing a tax return every year. It's a good idea to do this as soon as you go freelance but you have up until 5 October in your business's second tax year. That means if you started freelancing on 1 January 2021, you have until 5 October 2022 to register for self-assessment.

You can register online at: www.gov.uk/log-in-file-self-assessment-tax-return/register-if-youre-self-employed

One of the requirements of being a sole trader is that you must include your name and business name (if you have one) on official paperwork, like invoices and letters. You can trade under your own name as a sole trader or you can choose another name for your business. If you want to trade under another name, it can't include 'limited', 'Ltd', 'limited liability partnership', 'LLP', 'public limited company' or 'plc', nor can it be the same as an existing trademark.

If you don't want others to use your business name, you can register it as a trademark at www.gov.uk/how-to-register-a-trade-mark/apply

How to set up as a limited company

There are a few steps for setting up as a limited company.

First, you have to choose a name for your business. Your name can't be the same as another registered company's name or a registered trademark and it must usually end in either 'Limited' or 'Ltd'. You can search the Companies House database to see if your name is already in use.

Then you need to appoint a director who, if you're working for yourself, will be you. You also need to appoint a shareholder, who again will be you.

When you register your company, you need a 'memorandum of association', which is a legal statement signed by all initial shareholders agreeing to form the company. (If you register your company online, you don't need to write your own memorandum of association as it will be created automatically.)

You also need 'articles of association', which are written rules about running the company. You can either write your own and upload them when you register your company, or use standard articles which are available at www.gov.uk/guidance/model-articles-of-association-for-limited-companies

Once you have all your documents in place, you need to register the company with Companies House and HMRC, which costs £12 and can be done online at www.gov.uk/limited-company-formation/register-your-company

An accountant can also help you form and register your limited company, as can some self-employment services like the online accountancy firm Crunch and the mobile bank Tide.

Chapter summary: Setting Up

Start your self-employment journey off on the right foot by learning what rights you have, picking a job title that suits your working style and structuring your business in a way that makes financial sense for you.

Pick your own job title: When you work for yourself, you get to choose your job title. Freelancer, side-hustler, micro business owner, entrepreneur – the choice is yours. Take practical considerations into account when deciding how to refer to yourself but also think about your identity as a worker.

Freelancers have rights. Know them: While freelancers don't have the same rights as employees, they *are* protected against discrimination, health and safety violations and late payments. We're also entitled to a pension and other state benefits. Know what your rights are so that you can advocate for yourself should a client breach them.

Structure your business: You have two options for your freelance business: running it as a sole trader or setting up a limited company. The latter means your business is a separate entity from you. Which structure is right for you will depend on your personal circumstances, so spend some time researching your options. Remember, you can always go down the sole trader route and then start a limited company later on.

FREELANCER STORY

Sian Meades-Williams (@SianySianySiany) – freelance writer, editor and newsletter expert

I finished university and I didn't know what I was doing. As helpful as an English Literature degree is, no one ever told me what career I could get with my qualification. I didn't know how to go off and be a writer. This was pre-Twitter, when the internet wasn't full of resources and information about freelancing. It just didn't exist. So, when I got offered a job to edit a new lifestyle website in London, I jumped at it. Unfortunately, that job lasted three months. I was unceremoniously let go in the middle of a Starbucks. It was mortifying and weird, and I had no idea what to do next.

I'd never learned to freelance. I didn't really even know that's what I was doing when I started. I was just trying to be incredibly scrappy until someone I knew gave me a contact for someone else who might be commissioning, and that's how I eventually landed my first writing gig. I want to say it spiralled from there but it genuinely didn't because I don't think I was treating freelancing as a business. If I'm really honest, I don't think I did for years. I was just pitching when I needed to and saying yes to every piece of work that came my way.

After a while, I realised that I wanted to create something of my own. I saw a gap in the market for a website – or blog, as we used to call them – that covered food and design. What I didn't realise was I was taking the very first steps to setting up one of the first lifestyle blogs in the UK.

I launched Domestic Sluttery with some friends and once that went live, things snowballed really quickly. The money from the blog was adding enough to my salary that I could freelance around it and I could do half and half. That's how I learned how to edit a website, be a writer and an editor, and create something that was totally my own. It wasn't until then that I started making something that really felt like mine. I think I'd always been kind of fumbling my way through. And now that's the bit that I love about freelancing.

What I call myself changes every day. On my mortgage application, I'm an editor and author because it sounds more authoritative than 'freelance writer'. Sometimes I'm an editor; sometimes I'm a freelance writer; sometimes I'm an entrepreneur. Sometimes I'm a person having a nap in the middle of the day! They are just labels. And all I have to do is say, 'I'm Sian and this is what I do.'

CHAPTER TWO

Your First Clients

My first freelance contract didn't come from a LinkedIn post, a networking event or even a job board. It came through someone I'd once shared a tent with at a music festival on the Isle of Wight in the late 2000s.

In the ten years since Vicky and I drank cider out of cans in a muddy field, we had both become journalists. Our paths took us on different courses but we reconnected when I lost my job in 2017 and reached out to Vicky. She was working as an editor at a digital magazine at the time and introduced me to her boss, who swiftly asked me if I could cover someone on the team while they went on holiday. That three-week stint of work was the confidence boost (and pay cheque) I needed to feel like maybe this freelancing thing might just work out for me.

The sooner you can get your first freelance client, the sooner working for yourself will actually feel doable. In this chapter, I'm going to walk you through my go-to techniques for finding your first clients. Over the following pages, I'll walk you through how to use your existing network to find your first piece of work, and in later chapters you'll learn how to develop longer-term strategies for bringing in clients over the long haul.

First, though, I need to introduce a *little* bit of business jargon because there's a technical word for how you find clients. It's called ... marketing and sales. I can already feel you pulling away but stay with me! I know that many people find promoting and selling difficult at best and downright repulsive at worst. The reality is, however, that every business needs to market itself and sell to customers and your freelance business is not an exception. The difference is that a large company has an entire sales team whereas you *are* the sales team when you work for yourself. This chapter will help you get comfortable with the idea of marketing and selling because, as much as we might not like it, there's no way to avoid it. Sales and marketing are so important, in fact, that there are two more chapters on them later on in this book. I'm going to make a bold claim and say that by the end of this chapter, I'll have changed your mind about marketing and sales and helped you find a way to actually enjoy the process.

I want to start by asking you to think about a positive experience you've had when being sold to. A time when you walked away not only with the goods in hand but feeling happy about parting with your money. If you can't think of one, let me tell you about a recent experience I had being sold a second-hand car.

When we think of the worst kind of salespeople, second-hand car dealers are often at the top of the list. So I went into the purchase with my head filled with the stereotype of sleazy salesmen upselling cars completely unsuitable for my lifestyle. But that wasn't my experience with Rachel at all. I told her that I needed a car big enough to fit my lively Labrador in and it needed to be compliant with the emission regulations in London. I already had something in mind and she walked me through all the other options I had. She let me test drive a few cars alone so I could just focus on whether I actually liked them without her running commentary. She didn't push me at all. I went around to a few other dealerships but ended up going back to Rachel and buying a car from her. It was the biggest purchase I'd ever made and I felt really good about it.

Why was that such a good experience? Because Rachel actually *listened* to me. When I told her I needed a car that could fit a big dog, she showed me SUVs and estates. When I told her I was still figuring out my budget and would need some time to decide, she didn't push me to make a call on the spot. More importantly, Rachel let me come to the decision to buy a car from her *on my own*. People do want to buy things; they just don't want to feel like they're being sold to. I wanted to buy a car but I wanted to buy the one I'd decided was right for me. When you start to think of good sales as an exercise in listening, it suddenly becomes about people and not products. And that's the secret.

If you're still not convinced, let's unpack what it really is about sales that so many of us hate. Countless freelancers have told me over the years that they delayed launching their businesses out of embarrassment about what people would think of them. Some can't stand the thought of selling goods or services to people they don't know, feeling more comfortable with people who already know they're good at what they do. Others, however, are fine selling to 'strangers' but don't like the thought of friends and family seeing – and perhaps judging – what they're doing when they put themselves, and their professional talents, out there. After all, before I worked for myself, it's not like I wanted my parents to come into the office and watch over my shoulder as I worked.

Let's take a moment to understand why you may feel embarrassment about striking out on your own. Embarrassment is what's known as a self-conscious emotion. It happens when you become conscious of a fear (which can be real or imagined) that what you're doing deviates from social norms. In other words, you become worried about what people will think of you. It's important to remember that embarrassment can happen regardless of whether the situation is positive or negative. You could feel just as embarrassed by forgetting someone's name as by someone complimenting you in public. When you think about embarrassment in these terms, it's no wonder you may feel embarrassed about starting your freelance career. Self-employment is still not the norm. It means going against the grain and not doing what's expected of us. Even if you're really excited by the prospect of working for yourself, you can still feel embarrassed by it. The advice in this chapter will help you overcome feelings of embarrassment and fear about starting and selling your freelance business.

In this chapter, you'll learn:

- How to understand who your clients are
- Why people want to hire you
- Strategies for finding your first clients
- How to handle client relationships

Finding Your First Clients

Your network is crucial to the success of your freelance business from day dot. Your first clients will most likely come from connections you already have and your future clients will come from connections you continue to make. The easiest and fastest way to land your first client is by using whatever resources you already have access to – just like I did with Vicky at the start of my freelance career. Even if you're completely new to freelancing, your industry and even the workforce all together, you *do* have an existing network. It may not be expansive (yet!) but you do have a place from which to start building.

Now, I already know what you're thinking. You might believe me when I say we're all more connected than we realise, it's just that using those connections makes you feel gross. Let me ask you this: if someone came to you and asked for help (within reason!), would you give it to them? Of course you would. Well, that's networking! Networking doesn't – and shouldn't – have to be a greasy pole because authentic networking is simply helping other people out. The golden rule with networking is to ask someone for something that's reasonable. If you would reciprocate were the ask reversed then there's nothing to feel icky about.

Traditional business books often talk about 'exploiting your networks'. You'll hear networking described in transactional terms, like 'I'll scratch your back and you scratch mine.' That's where the negative connotations about networking come from. Instead, I want to introduce you to a more palatable way of thinking about networking.

I think of a network like a two-tiered cake. At the top are your closest connections and underneath is the larger layer of your secondary connections. You need to slice through the top layer to reach that big bottom layer. As for who sits on which layer, let's start with the top tier.

These are friends and people with whom you've worked on a daily basis. The litmus test for these people is whether you could call them up out of the blue to ask them for a favour without it being weird. The next layer are people you have either interacted with a couple of times before or with whom you share a top-tier mutual connection. It would be OK for you to email these people directly or to have someone introduce you to them.

Start by making a list of your top-tier connections. Write down friends as well as people you've worked with in the past. To help you focus your list as much as possible, think about people who work at companies you'd like to freelance for (even if they aren't in the right department) as well as people who work in your industry. The aim of putting this list together is to have a go-to resource to help land your first client.

Once you have your list, go through it and, next to each person's name, write down exactly what you're going to ask them when you reach out for help. Broadly speaking, in this situation there are three things you can ask of someone you know: you can directly ask them for work; you can ask them to introduce you to someone else who might be able to give you work; or you can ask for their advice on how to go about finding work. This step is important because if you want good results, you're going to have to tailor your request, spelling out clearly and directly how someone can help. A general 'copy-and-paste' approach won't work here.

For example:

- If you just started your freelance floristry business and your friend is getting married, your ask might be to do the flowers at their wedding.

- If you're starting your freelance workplace wellbeing training programme and your friend works for a large company, your ask might be an introduction to their HR department.
- If you're launching your freelance copywriting business and your friend has been doing it for years, your ask might be how they find their clients.

Once you've worked your way through that first tier, it's time to move on to the second one. Some of this list will be comprised of people your first-tier connections introduced you to, while others will be people you know just about well enough to email directly.

Generally speaking, the main reason you want to connect with second-tier contacts is to ask for work. The simplest way to approach the conversation is to just tell them that you've gone freelance and you're available for work. If you're not sure what to say, use this template as a guide:

Hello Jo Second-Tier Contact,

I'm getting in touch to share some exciting professional news, which is that I'm now freelance. Having worked at My Previous Company for five years, I've decided I can better serve clients as an independent contractor. I really enjoyed working with you on That Previous Project and would love to find a way for us to continue working together.

These are the types of things I can help you out with:
- *Writing website copy*
- *Designing logos and websites*
- *Developing content strategy*

More info is on my website [include a link!] or feel free to give me a call and we can discuss further.

I'm really excited about this new venture and would be thrilled for you to be a part of it.

Finding work online

Freelance jobs boards are a good place to start looking for initial clients. On the generic job sites, like Indeed.com and Monster.com, you can filter by contract type to only show results for freelance opportunities.

Freelance marketplaces are sites on which clients can advertise work that freelancers can bid for. I'm not a fan of these sites because often the rates are lower than working directly with a client. There's also a race to the bottom in bidding, with clients looking for the cheapest labour, which pushes freelance rates down.

Specialist jobs boards are a better bet. These sites are usually run by industry insiders and many require advertisers to list their rates on the posting. You will also find sector-specific work on these sites which is more likely to lead to repeat opportunities. There is a list of these jobs boards in the directory on page 303.

How to use social media to find your first clients

How you use social media should be part of your long-term marketing strategy. I'll go into this in chapter six but I do have some tips for using social media to land your initial clients.

Social media as a search tool: Use it to find the right contact details. In some industries, it's the norm for people to make their job titles and email addresses public on their social media accounts. Journalists, for example, will have their email addresses in their Twitter bio so if you're looking to pitch to an editor you can find the right person to contact.

Broadcasting your availability: If framed well, social media can be a great place to let potential clients know you're looking for work. Rather than explicitly stating you need work, post about your availability to take on new clients or projects instead. You want to give an impression of opportunity rather than desperation.

Engage and connect: Start talking to the right people. Comment on people's LinkedIn posts, reply to people's tweets, contribute in Facebook group discussions. Just like with real-life networks, you get back as much as you put in with social media connections.

Show your work: Social media is fast becoming a real-time CV. Post about your work online, sharing links to projects you're proud of and any recent work you've done.

Use industry-specific social media sites: When we think about professional social media networks, the first one to come to mind is usually LinkedIn. While LinkedIn can be a powerful tool for many freelancers, there are also a host of industry-specific sites that you can use:

- GitHub for coders
- Behance and Dribble for designers
- Flickr and Unsplash for photographers
- Vimeo for videographers
- Contently for writers
- The Dots for creatives

The half-hour LinkedIn makeover

For most freelancers, LinkedIn can be a gold mine for new clients. When my podcast co-host Tiffany Philippou started her freelance coaching business, she posted an update on LinkedIn and landed her first three clients within 24 hours.

The following tips will take you about half an hour and will give your LinkedIn profile the spruce-up it needs to help you find clients:

- **Use a proper photo:** It doesn't have to be a corporate headshot but choose a picture that looks professional.
- **Write a clear and descriptive one-line bio:** Instead of 'wordsmith', be specific: 'Copywriter with ten years' experience in health, consumer technology and personal finance'.
- **Update your summary:** Your summary is your cover letter. It's where you show prospective clients how you can help them. Spell this out clearly by explaining how you work with clients, what results you can achieve and what skills you have. If you want a guide for what to write, feel free to look at my LinkedIn page as an example: www.linkedin.com/annacodrearado
- **Post your availability:** Write a post detailing that you've gone freelance and what type of work you're looking for at the moment. Use the template on page 31 as a guide.
- **Use the built-in tools:** Check the 'available for work' button is marked 'on' or write in your summary page that you're currently accepting new clients.

A Primer on Dealing with Clients

Once you start landing your first clients, you'll soon face the subsequent challenge of learning how to manage them. Whether you're a photographer dealing with face-to-face customers or a virtual assistant communicating over email, good client relationships are crucial to the success of your business. Here are my tips for starting off on the right foot with your client relationships.

Make their priorities your priorities

Clients are happiest when they feel like they're being taken care of and listened to. If you want a long and happy relationship with your clients, make it a priority to understand what's most important to them. Simply asking them direct questions like 'what's your priority with this project?', 'what are your expectations?' or 'what are you struggling with at the moment?' will help you understand why they hired you and what they want from your working relationship. If you're nervous about asking these sorts of questions, remember that you're doing yourself and your potential clients a favour by ensuring you actually understand what it is they're looking for.

Communicate, communicate, communicate

Communicating well with clients doesn't mean sending them an email update every day. Unless, of course, that's what they're expecting from you. The secret to good communication is understanding what exactly this means to the other person. A good practice to establish is, once you've secured your project or piece of work, to include details of when the client will next hear from you. If you're working on a longer-term or ongoing project, make sure you have an upfront conversation about communication – some will expect regular catch-up calls, while others will only want to hear from you when the work is completed.

Don't forget about feedback

There's a double-edged sword when it comes to feedback in a business of one. When you're the boss, it becomes all too easy to slip into thinking that any time you don't like something, you can just turn away from it or pretend it didn't happen. While this is great for walking away from work situations that don't serve you, it can also mean you forget to take on board important, constructive feedback. If a client gives you well-intended feedback that's perhaps hard to hear but ultimately helpful, graciously accept it.

Be aware of scope creep

Most clients don't have experience of being freelance and, as such, make what can feel like unreasonable requests. One of the most common ways this happens is through what's known as scope creep – the tacking on of additional work to an already agreed upon project. You'll spot scope creep when a client says to you, 'Could you just …' and then asks for additional work outside of the parameters of the project. For the most part, clients do this because they are busy or stressed or simply don't realise that what they're asking is cheeky. In these situations, don't be afraid to gently push back by explaining how long their request will take or why you're not the right person to do it. More often than not, they'll apologise and back down – or in some cases pay you for your additional time.

Learn how to say no

Inevitably, there will be some clients with whom you just don't gel. You might find that no matter how much you try, they don't respect your professional boundaries or they downright mistreat you in some way. Give yourself permission to turn down work, end a client relationship or take whatever steps you need to in order to protect yourself in these instances. I go into more detail about boundaries and difficult client situations in later chapters.

Chapter Summary: Your First Clients

The majority of freelancers find their first clients through their existing network. Rather than faffing with a website, when you first start out, spend your time connecting with contacts you already have and develop good habits for managing those relationships early on.

The importance of networking: Proactively reach out to your existing contacts for work, being clear on your ask and tailoring your approach.

Find your first clients through social media: Social media can be a great place to show off your portfolio and to search for your initial clients.

Build good client relationships: Once you find your first clients, keep them by practising good communication habits and professional boundaries.

FREELANCER STORY

Vicky Simmons (@meanmail) – founder of Mean Mail

Just before I set up my current business, Mean Mail, I took on a freelance contract with a previous employer. It made me realise how important it is to leave doors open for yourself and to leave on good terms. When you freelance, your growth happens almost in dog years. You move from client to client and end up becoming a really fast learner. It's definitely exhausting being a freelancer because it feels like you're always performing and trying to be your best work self. At the same time, you really reap the rewards in terms of higher pay and exciting projects.

Before I launched a product-based business, I worked as an advertising creative. I loved it because I love ideas and I really thrive off that sort of work. However, it took me over a decade to realise that it's not simply a case of good ideas being the ones that get made. In fact, more often than not, what gets made comes down to politics, ego and power. I also realised that there's no such thing as job security. Being in a full-time role lulls you into the belief that the job is there for as long as you want it but that's just not true. Things can be pulled out from underneath you in an instant. Once I understood all this, I just wanted to quit

---

and do my own thing, which is how I ended up launching a greetings card business.

In a world that is already full of products, it was really important to make sure what I created had a strong design aesthetic. I created Mean Mail because I felt like there were no cards that were sarcastic and humorous with a really strong design aesthetic. I love the contrast between the really colourful pastels and the less than saccharine messages. It was important to me to have a high attention to detail because that's what makes receiving the card so special.

Launching a business selling physical products can be daunting because if something goes wrong, it can be harder to correct than with digital products. If you make a typo on a digital product, you can fix it and reupload it straight away. There are a lot more variables that are out of your control with physical items. But I definitely think there's always going to be a place for physical products. It's just about making it feel special and creating the best possible experience that you can deliver with the product. There's always going to be room for special things that you can hold in your hands.

CHAPTER THREE

Day-to-day Finances

When I started freelancing, managing my daily finances was a real struggle. Going from a monthly pay cheque to irregular income was painful in unexpected ways. Despite priding myself on being good at budgeting when I worked in staff roles, after I became self-employed, I realised that I needed to re-learn the art of personal finance. The problem wasn't so much the amount I was earning but how and when I got paid. I could no longer rely on things that I used to take for granted, like money appearing in my bank account each month without me having to ask for it. It's hard doing a monthly budget when you don't know how much money you're going to make that month.

There were also new problems to deal with, like how tax actually works and how to put money aside for it. I understood the abstract concept that I would have to pay my tax bill myself but I didn't know the mechanics of how that was going to work. How much of my earnings was I supposed to save and where was I meant to keep that money? I never used to think about national insurance contributions and suddenly they were on my mind all the time. After initially burying my head in the sand, I soon found that the best way to manage my money was to embrace the business side of freelancing. That meant getting comfortable with terms like cash flow (the amount of money that comes in and out of your business) and putting aside time every week to check my finances were in order. The tired cliché that admin is boring does freelancers no favours. I now prioritise my admin because I've come to see it as a necessary part of my freelancing. In fact, I've stopped calling it admin altogether and instead think of it as 'operations', the term for the part of a business that keeps things running. It's like the engine of your freelancing business – without it you'll stall.

An unexpected side effect of taking a proactive interest in the business side of freelancing has been the boost it's given my confidence when it comes to money. Before, I would feel uncomfortable every time I had to talk about money with a client, which when you're self-employed can be on a daily basis. I now feel less awkward when I'm chasing invoices or asking for a higher rate because I'm doing so on behalf of my business. I realise now that I had previously used the fact that my line of work is creative as an excuse for hiding from the numbers. I might not have formal business training but, like all creatives, I can problem solve and figure things out. As I'll explain in this chapter, you definitely don't need a business degree to do your taxes or to stay on top of your finances. All you need is a willingness to learn. There's a nerdy saying in the business world that 'cash flow is king'. It means that your most important financial vital sign is how much money you actually have on hand. And the only way to make sure you have more money coming in than going out is to roll up your sleeves and get acquainted with all aspects of your money.

In this chapter, you'll learn:

- How to get paid for your freelance work

- How to build good financial systems and habits
- How to stay on top of your taxes

Getting Paid

Bank accounts

So, you want to get paid. As obvious as it sounds, first you'll need a bank account. Get off on the right foot by having a completely separate one for your business finances. This account will receive all the money that you make through freelancing and you can also use it to pay for any business expenses you incur. Separating your finances out like this makes it much easier to keep track of the money coming in and out of your freelancing business. Not only can you see at a glance how much income you have in your account, but also, when it comes to doing your tax return, you won't have to pick through your Deliveroo and Netflix charges to find your expenses.

The type of bank account you need to open will vary depending on the kind of freelancing you do. If you are registered as a limited company, you **must** have a specific business bank account – you can't use a personal current account. Sole traders on the other hand are not required to do this and could open a second current account for their freelance income. However, be mindful that many banks' terms and conditions restrict the use of current accounts for business purposes.

It used to be the case that new freelancers were put off opening a business account because the high street banks charged hefty fees for them but a slew of new online banks have sprung up in the last few years that offer free or low-cost business accounts. Starling, Monzo, Tide, Coconut and ANNA Money all offer business bank accounts specifically for sole traders, freelancers and small businesses.

Before opening your account, think about what you'll need from it. Some business accounts offer additional services such as invoicing and bookkeeping, as well as business loans and overdrafts.

Start a system for keeping track of your cashflow

Once you have your bank account set up, you need a system for keeping track of the money coming in and out of it. This is called bookkeeping and I promise it's not as dull as it sounds, especially when you think about how staying on top of it will mean you're not kept up at night worrying about your finances.

HMRC requires all self-employed people to keep records of their business income and expenses. It's not optional. How you keep your records will vary depending on whether you're registered as a sole trader or as a limited company.

Keeping records as a sole trader

If you are a sole trader, you need to keep a record of your business income and expenses for your tax return, as well as your personal income. This includes any income you make from renting out a room in a property you own, interest on savings or returns on investments (declaring personal income on your self-assessment tax return applies to everyone, whether you're self-employed or not). To keep your records, you'll typically use what's known as a 'cash basis accounting method'. This means that you only record the income or expense when you actually receive the money or pay a bill. In other words, you will not need to pay income tax on money that you have invoiced but not received in the financial year.

For example: the 2021/22 financial year runs from 6 April 2021 to 5 April 2022. If you invoiced someone on 15 March 2022 but did not receive the money until 1 May 2022, you record this income for the 2022/23 tax year.

You can use the cash basis accounting method if you're a sole trader and have a turnover of £150,000 or less a year. The alternative is to use accruals, which recognises income as soon as you raise an invoice for it, even if it hasn't been paid yet. If you're doing your own bookkeeping, just make sure whichever accounting method you use is consistent.

Keeping records for a limited company

If you are registered as a limited company, you must keep detailed records. These include: all the money spent by the company (e.g. receipts, petty cash books and orders), all the money received by the company (e.g. invoices, contracts and sales books), details of assets owned by the company (e.g. laptops, phones and equipment), as well as details about the directors and shareholders of the company (e.g. addresses and dates of birth).

Most freelancers who are registered as a limited company choose to hire an accountant to keep these records for them as they are a lot more involved than what's required of a sole trader and HMRC heavily penalises companies for getting it wrong. In this chapter, I'll explain what you need to know if you plan to do it yourself.

How to keep good records

Regardless of whether you're a sole trader or limited company and whether you use an accountant or not, you'll need a system for keeping your records. As a freelancer, there are two core things you need your bookkeeping system to do: track incoming payments and log business expenses. Ideally, you want a system that does that and is easy to use, doesn't require any accounting knowledge and is digital.

A spreadsheet and a shoebox

The cheapest way to keep track of your freelancing finances is with a simple spreadsheet that records your income and expenses.

On one tab you want to record your income. Include the invoice number, the date you submitted the invoice, the due date, the client's name, the project details, the amount and whether the invoice has been paid yet.

Then use another tab to keep track of your expenses. Include the date, the description of the item and a short note about why this counts as an allowable expense (e.g. if it's a train ticket, 'travel for offsite client meeting' will do). It's also a good idea to include an expense category that matches up with the ones HMRC approves (there are some examples of what you can and can't expense on page 65).

You'll also need to keep hold of your receipts, either by stuffing them in a shoebox the old-fashioned way or by taking pictures of them and storing them in a file on your phone or computer (and backing them up!). Remember that whichever way you decide to store your receipts, by law you're required to keep your business records for at least five years after submitting your tax return to HMRC.

Bookkeeping software

If you don't want to use a spreadsheet, you can opt for book-keeping software instead. In the past, this meant buying an expensive and complicated package you had to install onto your computer, but now there are lots of companies offering affordable, cloud-based systems. QuickBooks, Xero, FreeAgent and Crunch all offer easy-to-use software that you don't need an accounting qualification to use. These services do charge fees, but don't forget that the cost counts as an allowable business expense against your taxes (I'll be covering everything you need to know about expenses later in this chapter).

In exchange for your money you get an easier life. Book-keeping software can do a lot more than a simple spreadsheet, unless you're an Excel formula wizard. For example, most services include an invoice generator, which makes it easier and faster to send invoices and keep track of the payments; many also offer late payment chasing features. They often include an app for scanning in pictures of your receipts, so no need for the shoebox, as well as the ability to integrate with your bank account so they can pull in your spending automatically. Most helpfully, though, if you use bookkeeping software, you can see at a glance how much money you've made in a given month, making it much easier to keep on top of your budgeting. If you end up switching your book-keeping software at any point, or stop using it, remember to download all your data first so you don't lose it. Also be mindful to pick software that's compliant with HMRC's recent Making Tax Digital initiative to take the tax system fully online.

However you decide to keep track of your income and expenses, the most important thing is to find a system that actually works for you. It's like exercise: if you hate the tread-mill, you'll never work out, but if you like running outdoors, you'll do it. The same goes for your finances.

Invoicing for your work

As a freelancer, gone are the days of money magically appearing in your bank account each month. To actually get paid for your work, you first have to send an invoice to your client, who will then pay you, usually via a bank transfer.

Most bookkeeping software comes with an invoice template as standard. All you have to do is input the details into the invoice generator and it makes one for you; many will also even send it on your behalf.

If you want to make your invoices yourself, you can do this quite easily in Word, Excel or Google Sheets. All three provide free templates, or you can easily make one from scratch. You need to include the date, the invoice number, your name, address and contact details, your client's name and address (and your contact there if the details are different), the amount due, a description of the work, the payment due date and your bank details. Some clients will ask for additional information on invoices; pre-empt delays by including your national insurance number, full bank details (such as bank address and SWIFT/BIC code) and tax-payer number upfront.

Invoicing habits

A good habit to develop is invoicing once a week. Block out an hour each week for sending invoices, checking on incoming payments and chasing any late payers.

The big advantage of invoicing like this rather than on an ad hoc basis is that it helps keep things super organised. It's easy to lose track of invoices if you're sending them as and when work comes in. By dedicating a time slot to invoicing and checking on payments only, you know exactly where you stand with your cash flow each week and it's easier to spot when something is overdue and needs chasing.

This can also help regulate your payments because if you send off invoices in a batch, you should be receiving the corresponding payments together as well.

Late payments

Late, slow and no payments are the scourge of freelancing. Not only do they affect cash flow but they can lead to personal financial trouble and are the number one reason freelancers go out of business. Legislation is slowly trying to catch up, but until that happens there are some things you can do to help yourself.

Know your rights

The Late Payment of Commercial Debt (Interest) Act gives self-employed workers in the UK the right to claim interest and debt recovery costs if another business is late in paying them.

A payment becomes late after the agreed payment date has passed. If you do not agree a payment date, the law says the payment is late 30 days after either the customer receives the invoice or you deliver the goods or provide the service (whichever is later).

If a business is late paying, you can charge what's known as statutory interest, which is an annual interest rate of 8%, plus the Bank of England base rate (which is currently 0.10%).

For example: if you're owed £1,000 and the client is 50 days late in paying you, they would owe you £11 in interest. How this is calculated:

- The annual statutory interest is £81 (1,000 × 0.081 = 81)
- Divide £81 by 365 to get the daily interest: 22p a day (81 ÷ 365 = 0.22)
- After 50 days this would be £11 (50 × 0.22 = 11)

However, you cannot claim statutory interest if a different rate of interest is stated in a contract, so make sure to read anything a client asks you to sign carefully.

You can also charge a fixed sum for the cost of recovering a late payment, on top of claiming interest for it.

The amount you're allowed to charge depends on the amount of debt and is set by the Late Payment of Commercial

Debt Act, so a company cannot contract out of it. These amounts are £40 for invoices up to £1,000, £70 for invoices over £1,000, and £100 for invoices over £10,000.

Payment terms

It's important to note that while the Late Payment of Commercial Debt Act offers provisions for freelancers and entitles them to claim a late payment fee, when you can claim that fee will depend on whether you agreed payment terms with the client in advance of doing the work.

There's a common misconception that stating your payment terms on your invoice means these are legally binding. In fact, you have to establish these terms prior to carrying out the work. If you do not have a contract with your client, or have not agreed the payment terms in advance, this is automatically 30 days by law. But, for example, if you have signed a contract that says payment terms are 90 days, you then cannot try to claim a late payment fee after 30 days.

It's a very good habit to check what the client's payment terms are as some large companies operate 90-day, or even 120-day, payment terms.

Once you've agreed on the payment terms, which can be done in a contract or over email, include a paragraph at the bottom of your invoice that clearly outlines them as well.

Payment terms are [A] days.

Please note that, in accordance with the Late Payment of Commercial Debt (Interest) Act 1998, a fixed sum of £[B] for the cost of recovering a late commercial payment will become due in the event that this invoice is not paid on or before the due date. A revised invoice including this late payment fee will be issued in the event this invoice becomes overdue; and starting from the day following the due date on this invoice, late payment interest will start accruing on the overdue payment at [C]%, being the statutory rate of 8% plus the Bank of England base rate, currently [D]%. Invoices will be updated weekly to reflect the accrued interest.

- 'A' should be the agreed payment days for your work in your contract. If you do not have a contract with your client and/or have not agreed the payment days in the contract, this is automatically 30 days by law.
- 'B' should be (in accordance with the law): £40 for invoices up to £1,000, £70 for invoices over £1,000, and £100 for invoices over £10,000.
- 'C' should be, if you don't have any different agreement on late payment interest, 8% plus 'D' (currently 0.10%, so it would be 8.10%). Remember that the statutory late payment interest due under the Late Payment of Commercial Debt (Interest) Act 1998 only applies if you have not included any provisions for late payment interest in your contract (if any) with your client. If you have a contract with your client which includes a reference to late payment interest at a specific rate, this is the rate you should use.
- 'D' should be the current Bank of England base rate (you can find this out by simply googling the current Bank of England base rate) – at the time of printing

this was 0.10%, but this can change so it is worth checking before you issue an invoice.

Oversupply information

As mentioned on page 49, different clients may ask for additional information on your invoice. Any time a client asks for a piece of information you haven't already supplied, start including that as standard on all your invoices going forward.

After you've sent your invoice, ask for confirmation of its receipt and that you have included all the relevant information on it.

Chase as soon as money is late

Don't wait until you need the money to chase it. Get in the habit of chasing late payments as soon as they are overdue, not just when you're in the red. Once a payment is past due, you are owed that money and entitled to a late payment fee, regardless of whether you need that money now or not. Having a robust system (as outlined on page 49) for invoicing is the best way to keep on top of late payments. This way, you know exactly who owes you what, when it's supposed to be coming in and when it's late.

What to do if you can't get your money

If your payment has gone overdue, there are steps you can take to get it paid.

Start with the person who assigned the work. Write them an email, keeping it as neutral as possible, that seeks to find out what they did with your invoice and when.

> *Dear XXX,*
>
> *I'm getting in touch to check on my outstanding payment. I'd really appreciate any help you can give in figuring out where the holdup is for this payment. Would you be able to confirm the date you processed my invoice at your end? Is there a contact in the accounts department I can speak with about this directly?*

From there, your next step is to speak with the accounts department. Try to get them on the phone, as often, in my experience, they ignore emails. When you speak with them, there's really only one question you need to ask: *What else do you need from me to expedite this payment?* More often than not, an invoice gets delayed because of a piece of missing information and if you can clear that up, you have a chance of getting an expected payment date for the invoice during the call. Remember to follow up with an email so that you have a paper trail of your correspondence.

If you've exhausted those avenues, if a client is ignoring your attempts to reach them or if they are refusing to pay you altogether, your next step is to involve a third party. If you are a member of a union, they will be able to help you recoup your money. There's a list of unions who offer support to freelancers in the directory on page 303.

A free option available to all freelancers is the Small Business Commissioner, a government service that handles cases of late payments. Note that the Small Business Commissioner currently only works with large organisations. It does not handle cases involving freelancers claiming from small businesses.

You can also take the company to the small claims court, which involves making a claim online and paying court fees. The fee is a sliding scale, depending on the amount you're claiming for. To give you an idea, the fee for claims up to £300 is £25, and £185 for amounts between £3,000 and £5,000. If you win the case, you may be able to claim the fees back. (For more on what to do when things go wrong, see chapter 11.)

International payments

If you do any work for international clients, getting paid can be tricky.

Paying tax on work done for international clients depends on where you're registered as a tax resident and also where the work was performed. If you're a UK tax resident, you'll normally pay UK income tax on your foreign income. If you've actually performed the work abroad, you may also be taxed in the foreign country. For example, a freelance virtual assistant who's a UK tax resident and does a piece of work for an American company from home will only pay tax to HMRC and not to the US tax authorities. However, if you're a videographer and UK tax resident and go and shoot the Australian Open, you will have to pay Australian tax and then claim tax relief in the UK. If you're in any doubt about which tax authorities you owe money to, speak with your accountant.

In terms of receiving the money, you have a few options. The easiest way is via an international wire transfer direct into your bank account. This option, however, often incurs hefty international transfer fees. While these fees do count as a deductible expense on your tax return, it's best to either ask your clients to cover these costs or to seek a lower-cost option.

There are now a number of companies that offer alternative international banking options. One of the market leaders in this area is TransferWise. It offers a currency transfer service and also local currency accounts, which can be helpful if you regularly work with international clients.

Doing Your Own Taxes

The most painful part of freelancing is undoubtedly doing your own taxes. Unlike when you work for a company and tax is deducted directly from your pay cheque, when you're self-employed it's on you to deal with your tax bills.

What types of tax you need to pay and how much will vary depending on the amount you earn and whether you're registered as a sole trader or as a limited company. As outlined in chapter one, tax implications are often the deciding factor for whether someone would choose to register as a sole trader or limited company.

Tax for sole traders

Your rate of income tax as a sole trader is the same as for employees; the only difference is that you have to pay the bill yourself by filing a self-assessment to HMRC.

As a sole trader, you pay income tax on your profits, which means you only pay tax on the money you make freelancing, minus your business expenses (more on expenses on page 65). You also need to pay national insurance contributions, which help you build up your state pension entitlement and fund welfare services like the NHS. NI contributions often catch first-time freelancers out so don't forget about them.

The amount of income tax you pay is dependent on how much of your income is above the personal allowance and which tax band the rest of your income falls into.

For the financial year 2020/21, the personal allowance is £12,500, which means you only start paying tax on the money you make above that amount.

If you claim marriage allowance or blind person's allowance, your personal allowance may be bigger. If your income is over £100,000, your personal allowance will be smaller.

Once you've hit your personal allowance, you start to pay tax on the additional income depending on your tax rate. In England, Wales and Northern Ireland, there are three tax bands: the basic rate (20%), higher rate (40%) and additional rate (45%). The table below shows how much income falls into those bands.

These bands are marginal, which means you only pay the tax rate on the portion of your earnings that falls within that range. For example, if you earn £30,000 you do not pay tax on the first £12,500 and you pay 20% on the remaining £17,500. If you earn £60,000, you do not pay tax on the first £12,500, you pay 20% on £37,500 and 40% on the remaining £10,000.

Band	Taxable income	Tax rate
Personal Allowance	Up to £12,500	0%
Basic rate	£12,501 to £50,000	20%
Higher rate	£50,001 to £150,000	40%
Additional rate	over £150,000	45%

If you live in Scotland, there are five tax bands.

Band	Taxable income	Scottish tax rate
Personal allowance	Up to £12,500	0%
Starter rate	£12,501 to £14,549	19%
Basic rate	£14,550 to £24,944	20%
Intermediate rate	£24,945 to £43,430	21%
Higher rate	£43,431 to £150,000	41%
Top rate	over £150,000	46%

Not saving enough money to cover taxes is a very common issue many first-time freelancers face. On page 68, there are examples of how to save money for your tax bill.

Payments on account

Payments on account are advance payments towards your tax bill. If your self-assessment tax bill is over £1,000, then you must make these payments. The exception to this rule is if you've already paid more than 80% of what you earn through PAYE.

The way to get your head around payments on account is to understand that there are two key tax dates that sole traders need to be aware of each year – 31 January and 31 July. Most people know that 31 January is the deadline for submitting your tax return and paying your bill. This is also the date that your first payment on account is due, which is usually 50% of your next tax bill. The remaining 50% (the second payment on account) is then due on 31 July. HMRC assumes that your earnings for the current financial year will be the same as last year, so your payment on account is based on those figures.

This means that when you pay your 2020/21 bill on 31 January 2022, you also need to pay half of your bill for the 2021/2022 year. The other half of the 2021/22 bill will then be due on 31 July 2022. If, when you submit your 2021/2022 tax return on 31 January 2023, you haven't cleared your tax bill, you'll owe the remaining balance plus your next payment on account for 2022/2023. And so on.

HMRC does this to spread out the payments you owe but an unintended consequence is that it catches out those in their first year of freelancing, who weren't expecting the additional 50% on top of their bill. In theory, if you've been setting aside money for your taxes as you've earned, this shouldn't be a problem. This is because tax returns are due in arrears nine months after the end of the financial year, which means a payment on account roughly means paying *all* the tax you owe to date in one go.

For example, if you started freelancing in November 2020, you wouldn't have to pay tax until 31 January 2022, when the self-assessment for the 2020/21 tax year is due. However, you will also be making a payment towards half of the subsequent financial year on that date as well. That payment is towards the 2021/22 tax year, which is the current financial year and which you will have already done work in. For the sake of your own blood pressure, it's helpful to get your head around this fact, and remember that HMRC isn't trying to take money that you don't owe them anyway.

In reality, however, most freelancers struggle to save enough for their tax bill in their first year. There's a lot to get to grips with and tax is often the first thing that slips. As payments on account are calculated based on the last tax return you filed, they also become a problem if your profits drop. In which case, you'll end up paying a larger amount than what you actually owe in tax. If you think this might happen to you, you can contact HMRC to ask them to reduce your payments. Do speak to an accountant before doing this because if you underpay, HMRC will charge you interest.

If you're doing your tax return for the first time, you can work out an estimate of how much will be due by using HMRC's Ready Reckoner tool. Plug in your details and it will give you a figure for the total annual tax you will be liable for. Then, divide that amount by two and add it to your previous total to give you the full amount you'll owe, for your first complete tax year plus the first six months of the following tax year.

Summary of Tax for Sole Traders

- As a sole trader, you pay tax on your income, minus your allowable business expenses, via self-assessment to HMRC.
- Your rate of tax will vary depending on your income, between 20 and 45%.
- You must also pay national insurance contributions.
- Key dates to remember are January 31 for paying your tax bill and July 31 for making payments on account.

Tax for limited companies

While it might not seem like it after reading those tax band tables, tax for sole traders is relatively straightforward. It's much more complicated for limited companies. The flipside, however, is that once you get your head around it, it can be a lot more tax efficient.

The main tax you pay if you are a limited company is corporation tax, which is currently 19%. You pay it by filing a CT600 form with HMRC and the money is due nine months and one day after your accounting period ends. You also have to file abridged accounts to Companies House which are then made public on its website. These documents show some company details and a balance sheet but your income and expenditure are not on public record.

You pay this 19% corporation tax on whatever profit is left after you deduct your allowable expenses from the company's income. The rules for expenses are slightly different from those for sole traders in terms of how you record and claim them but the principle that an expense is allowable if it's 'wholly and exclusively' for business purposes is the same.

A key allowable expense that freelancers who run limited companies need to be aware of is their salaries. If you run a limited company you will typically draw a salary from it. This will lower the amount of corporation tax you pay.

Your salary is still liable for the same income tax as outlined on page 58 but because you set your own salary many freelancers opt for an amount that won't incur income tax or national insurance contributions. However, you need to make sure to set your salary high enough to earn you pension contributions. This is explained in more detail on page 234.

Many freelancers will top up their salaries by taking out dividends from their limited companies. Dividends are payments made from a company to its shareholders out of its profits. In the case of a limited company with you as its sole director (which is the case for most freelancers who run a limited company), that means payments you draw from your business after corporation tax.

If your dividends are over £2,000 (and assuming you've fully utilised your personal allowance) then you will have to pay income tax on them via self-assessment. The amount you need to pay on the remaining dividends depends on the amount of income.

	Taxable income	Tax rate
Basic rate	£2,000 to £37,500	7.5%
Higher rate	£37,501 to £150,000	32.5%
Additional rate	over £150,000	38.1%

Running a limited company can be more tax efficient than operating as a sole trader but administratively it's much more complicated. It's strongly advisable to hire an accountant to help make sure you stay on top of your tax responsibilities.

VAT

There's no point sugar-coating it, VAT is complicated. What I've outlined below isn't a guide to DIY VAT returns. Instead, it's intended to help you understand what VAT is, when you have to register for it and why you might consider doing so voluntarily.

Value Added Tax (VAT) is a tax charged on most goods and services in the UK and EU. To be 'registered for VAT' simply means you must charge VAT on the goods and services you sell. It also means that if you buy goods and services, you can claim the VAT on them back. If you're registered for VAT, you need to file a VAT return every three months to HMRC. Failure to do so incurs a penalty fee. Your bookkeeper or accountant can file your return for you, as can online accounting software. Note that from 1 April 2019, as part of the government's Make Tax Digital rules, you can only use HMRC-approved software to file your VAT return. You can check if your software is compatible at www.gov.uk/guidance/find-software-thats-compatible-with-making-tax-digital-for-vat

You must register for VAT if your VAT taxable turnover (all your sales that aren't VAT exempt) was more than £85,000 over the last 12 months, or if you expect your VAT taxable turnover to be more than £85,000 in the next 30-day period. There are also rules about registering for VAT if you sell goods or services that are exempt from VAT but you buy goods for more than £85,000 from EU VAT-registered suppliers.

If you meet any of these criteria, you need to register within 30 days. The above applies whether you're a sole trader or limited company. There's a misconception that VAT only applies to limited companies. Not only is VAT registration open to sole traders, they must register if they meet the above criteria.

You can also voluntarily register for VAT at any time. You're probably thinking, why would I do that given how complicated it is? Well, there are benefits to registering voluntarily, particularly in certain circumstances. To start with, you'll be able to reclaim the VAT you're charged when you buy goods and services for your business. If your clients are large, VAT-registered companies themselves, they'll be used to seeing prices inclusive of VAT and will be able to claim it back. In some industries, such as construction, VAT registration is regarded as more professional, in a similar vein to how limited companies are also seen as more credible.

Of course, voluntary VAT registration isn't for every business. In the first instance, as you can see from the above, it incurs significant additional admin. If your clients are not VAT registered themselves, charging them VAT makes you more expensive. You'll typically be adding 20% to their invoices, which they won't be able to claim back. An accountant will be able to help you decide whether voluntarily registering for VAT is right for you.

You can register for VAT online at www.gov.uk/vat-registration. You can also hire an accountant, or use online accounting software, to register on your behalf and handle your VAT returns for you. Most businesses opt to have an expert take care of their VAT returns for them.

Summary of Tax for Limited Companies

- As a limited company, you must pay corporation tax on the income your company makes after expenses and taxable allowance via a CT600 form to HMRC.

- If you draw a salary below the national insurance primary threshold, you do not have to pay income tax or national insurance contributions.
- You can claim allowable business expenses.
- You must also pay tax on any dividends you receive via a self-assessment form each year.

Expenses

Your freelance business will have various running costs. You can deduct some of these costs to work out your taxable profit as long as they're allowable expenses.

For example, if your invoices come to a total of £30,000, and you claim £10,000 in allowable expenses, you only pay tax on the remaining £20,000. This is known as your 'taxable profit'.

Costs you can claim as allowable expenses include: office costs (e.g. stationery, renting a desk or phone bills); travel costs (e.g. train and bus tickets, fuel and parking); staff costs (e.g. subcontractor costs and wages); things you buy to sell on (e.g. stock or raw materials); financial costs (e.g. insurance or bank charges and accountancy fees); costs of your business premises (e.g. heating, lighting and utilities); advertising or marketing (e.g. website costs); and training courses related to your business (e.g. refresher training and professional development courses).

The thing to remember with expenses is that they must be 'wholly and exclusively' for business purposes. This means that you can claim for the cost of buying bookkeeping software, going on a marketing training course or buying lunch while working for a client offsite. You cannot, however, claim for the clothes you wear while working from home.

If you work from home you can claim a proportion of your costs for things like heating, electricity, council tax, mortgage interest or rent and internet and phone bills. As with all expenses, you'll need to find a reasonable method of dividing your costs.

The example HMRC gives is for working out how much of your electricity bill you can expense if you work from home. Say you have four rooms in your home and use one of them as an office and your electricity bill for the year is £400. You could claim £100 as allowable expenses (£400 divided by 4). If you only worked one day a week from home, you could claim £14.29 as allowable expenses (£100 divided by 7).

Managing Your Money

By this point, hopefully you're more on top of your finances and have got your head around the dreaded tax bill. But even if *you've* got used to the fact that money comes in at different times of the month, the rest of the world operates on a monthly billing cycle. Rent, utilities and credit card bills are due each month, so how can you stay on top of the regular financial commitments when your income is irregular?

The sole trader 'salary'

As I outlined at the beginning of this chapter, it's a good idea to separate out your business and personal finances. If you do this, not only is it easier to manage your business finances, you can also pay yourself the equivalent of a monthly wage.

Start by doing a budget to work out your average monthly living costs. Include things that have to get paid each month like rent, utilities, groceries and any other regular bills you have, but also make sure to be realistic and include some money for things like going out, holidays and shopping.

Once you have an amount, set up an automated transfer to pay that amount into your personal account from your business one each month. You want to aim for an amount that seems manageable in relation to how much you earn but that will also comfortably cover your personal expenditure each month.

How much salary to take as a limited company

If you set up as a limited company, one of the ways to take money out of your business is by paying yourself a salary. If you take advantage of this then you do have a payday just as you would do if you worked for any other employer.

The important thing about drawing a salary as a limited company is to take an amount that works out to be the most tax efficient for you.

To start with, it's a good idea to keep your annual salary below the tax-free personal allowance, which for the tax year 2020/21 is £12,500. This means that you won't have to pay income tax on this amount.

Another thing to bear in mind with drawing a salary is how it impacts your qualifying years for the state pension. There is something known as the 'national insurance contributions primary threshold', which is an amount set each year by the government that triggers your liability to pay national insurance contributions.

In the 2020/21 tax year that amount is £9,500. If you draw a salary of this amount, you won't pay any tax on it but you will still accrue qualifying years for the state pension.

If an annual salary of £9,500 isn't enough to meet your personal expenditure, you can top up your earnings by taking dividends from your company. As these can be drawn monthly or quarterly, it should be straightforward to incorporate them into your budgeting.

Saving for tax

We've covered how to work out what tax you owe as a freelancer but what are some practical methods for making sure you're putting aside enough for it?

The pay-yourself-first method

The pay-yourself-first budgeting method is typically used by employees with a monthly pay cheque for long-term savings goals but freelancers can use it to put money aside for their taxes (as well as their other savings).

The principle is that you invest in your financial future by paying into your savings accounts before your daily spending, a.k.a. 'paying yourself first'. In practice, this means every time money comes into your account, you immediately transfer a percentage of it into a separate savings account. So when money comes into your account from an invoice payment, you immediately send a portion of it off to a separate savings account to save for your tax bill.

How much to transfer depends on your annual profits (your income minus your expenses). A rough rule of thumb for sole traders is to put aside 30% of your profit if you're a basic taxpayer and 40% if you're a higher taxpayer. This will account for your income tax as well as NI contributions. This method works best for freelancers with low costs, such as those who work from home and/or offer digital services. If you make physical products or have high production costs, your tax liability will be significantly lower than 30% of your profits and you may struggle to put that amount aside. Instead, you'll have to work out your gross profit (how much you made in sales minus what it cost you to make your goods) first.

Fixed regular transfer

Another option is to pay a fixed amount into a savings account each month via an automated transfer. This method works particularly well for sole traders who have a separate freelance income bank account and pay themselves a 'salary'. Money will accumulate in your business account and you'll find there is enough in there to pay a regular amount into a tax account.

The trick is to figure out an amount to transfer that's manageable but also will work out to roughly cover your tax liability by the end of the year. If you've been freelancing for a while, it's easier to predict this amount. Plus, if you have a good budget, this is actually easier than it might seem. You do have to remember to keep an eye on this account and to make sure the savings accumulating in it match up with your tax estimates.

Use a high-interest bank account

These are few and far between at the moment and the only ones on the market require you to lock in for a fixed period (usually a minimum of a year) but if you save your tax money in an account with a high-interest rate, the savings will work harder for you.

Automate as much as possible

Digital banks, including Monzo and Coconut, offer special tax features with their business accounts. Some will estimate how much tax you owe and others allow you to set a percentage to automatically put aside for tax every time you get paid.

Something to remember: you can never save too much for tax. In fact, if you do over-save for tax then filing your return should be a great time of year because there will be extra cash left over, like an end-of-year bonus.

Financial check-ins

The best way to stay on top of your day-to-day finances is to have your nose in your finances on a daily basis.

Set aside time for regular check-ins to make sure that all your money is on track and to avoid any nasty surprises. As well as weekly time for invoicing, it's a good idea to set aside monthly slots for checking on your tax situation. You can use HMRC's self-employed Ready Reckoner to make sure you're on track with your tax savings or if you have an accountant, you can check in with them. This is also a good time to make sure your expenses are in order, that you have copies (paper or digital) of all your receipts and that you've categorised them into some kind of comprehensive order in your bookkeeping system.

If you want to go the whole hog, do a more in-depth financial check-in once a quarter. You can check on your pension, investments, what percentage of your income is being made from your different revenue streams, which clients are paying the best, who is consistently paying late and anything else money related that you've been putting off and needs attention.

Chapter Summary: Day-to-day Finances

Set yourself up for financial success by building good money habits and creating organised systems. As dull as it might be, learning about tax, expenses and freelancer finances will save you big headaches down the line.

Get paid: Make your freelance life easier by separating your business and personal finances and picking the right bank account for your needs.

Develop good invoicing habits: Get into a good routine with your invoicing in order to avoid late payments.

Do your own taxes: Whether you're a sole trader or limited company, learn what the different taxes you're liable for are so that you can stay on top of your finances.

Spend money to save money: If you're really struggling to stay on top of your money, invest in a bookkeeper, an accountant or financial software to help you. It will be worth it for the peace of mind you'll get from it.

FREELANCER STORY

Tatiana Walk-Morris (@Tati_WM) – freelance features writer and journalist

I've always freelanced on the side in some capacity but I went full-time freelance in 2017. I did it because I'd had several jobs that just weren't a good fit for me. I decided to try freelancing because I wanted to be a journalist and a writer in some capacity. And I wanted to take a shot at working for myself because working for other people just was not working for me.

I make most of my income through journalism but I do take on some commercial work because it supplements my income. I find the ideology of 'selling out' to be very classist. I come from a single-parent household without generational wealth and I have a considerable amount of student loan debt. And honestly, just being a human is expensive. As much as I enjoy my job, it is a business; this is how I feed myself. You cannot ask freelance journalists to work for low wages and then tell them that they can't seek income elsewhere because that's 'selling out'. If you want to have this puritanical approach to freelance work, you need to pay for it. When I hear people question how I can do commercial work, it's because I think I deserve to live a good life and to be prepared for emergencies and I'm not going to wait for journalism to value me. If I don't stand up for what I'm worth and find clients who value me, it's going to make it harder for the Black female journalists that are coming up behind me and thinking that they have to accept less.

I've made more working for myself than I ever did working for somebody else. But the flip side to that is starting a freelance business is hard. I've had incidents where I've wanted to do something nice for myself and I couldn't, or an emergency came up for a loved one and I wasn't able to help out financially.

If a client I really want to work with hits me with a lowball rate, I run an evaluation process in my head. Is this a small publication held together by strings and love? Or is this a large publication that has a budget and they are devaluing me – is this actually insulting? I've come to understand that the clients that pay you less will stress you more. These situations made me realise that if I didn't advocate for myself, I wouldn't be able to free myself from the stress of not having a good level of savings.

I realised that I owed it to myself to pursue a life that comes with its own challenges but I find so rewarding. I'm glad that I've learned to trust myself more. Whether it's with regular employment or freelancing, if something doesn't feel right, lean into that and it'll save you a lot of grief later.

CHAPTER FOUR

Talking about Money

If you've ever heard me speak in public, chances are that I was talking about money. Money is one of my favourite subjects. You're not *supposed* to talk about it, so I love doing it. You'd think these talks would make people feel uncomfortable but I've found that the opposite is true. Every time I've spoken about money the response has been overwhelming gratitude. I can see the audience sit up whenever I talk about how much I earn and when I share freelancing rates at virtual events the chat box fills up with thank yous from the attendees.

I've not always been able to talk about money so easily. Early into my freelancing career, I landed a client that meant a really big deal to me. It was a company I'd admired for years, the kind of place you think, 'Gosh, wouldn't it be amazing to work for them?' Well, they offered me ongoing freelance work and I was over the moon about it. It was the first regular gig I'd landed. And then came the conversation about money. The terms of the work and how I would be paid were hurriedly explained to me over the phone and, in my excitement, I agreed to them on the spot. It took less than a week for me to realise that I'd agreed to something that made zero financial sense.

I'd felt so grateful for the work from a company I respected that I didn't know how to have a conversation about my compensation. I had the idea in my head that I should accept whatever offer this company made me because it was my dream gig. I didn't dare look greedy, ungrateful or insulting by quibbling over their offer. But the problem with being grateful and taking any offer you can get is that it starts to erode your self-worth. You must determine your value based on your skills and expertise, not allow it to be determined by those who under-value you.

Soon, I started to feel resentful towards the work I was doing. I quickly found myself overworked and under-paid, right back in the place I'd been when I'd worked as an in-house staffer in a thankless role from which I was eventually made redundant. I realised that by avoiding one awkward conversation about money at the start, I was suffering ongoing discomfort at the thought of how poorly I was being compensated. That experience taught me to *always* have the difficult money conversation upfront, no matter how much I want to avoid it. Financial stability isn't a destination, it's an ongoing practice that requires the right mindset and an understanding of the practical considerations. Your money goals will change over time, as will your needs and appetite for risk. I found that once I let go of the idea that how I manage my money has any moral value, it became a lot easier to distance myself from the emotions. It's now paramount to me that I'm comfortable talking about money so a fear of a conversation never again holds me back from getting what I'm worth.

In this chapter, I'm going to share what helped me become comfortable talking about money and by the end, you too will feel better equipped to stand up for your financial health and security.

In this chapter, you'll learn:

- How to change how you think about money
- Why we feel shame around money
- How to set your prices
- Tips for negotiating a fee

The Millionaire's Mindset

The late Thomas J. Stanley was an expert in rich people. His bestselling business book, *The Millionaire Next Door: The surprising secrets of America's wealthy*, lifted the lid on how millionaires actually accumulate their wealth. After surveying individuals with a net worth of over $1 million, Stanley found that the majority of millionaires don't drive flash cars or wear expensive watches. Instead they simply live within their means and spend a lot of their time budgeting.

'Wealth is more often the result of a lifestyle of hard work, perseverance, planning, and, most of all, self-discipline,' Stanley wrote. According to Stanley, becoming a millionaire is all about mindset and lifestyle. So much so that it's possible to become a millionaire while earning an average salary.

My own millionaire's mindset reminds me that no one gets rich by accident. You might stumble across a brilliant business idea but you won't just stumble across the money. That part always needs to be intentional, strategic and planned. I've seen this happen in my own freelance career. When I started working for myself, I began documenting the journey in a newsletter.

When I sent the very first email, from my mum's attic room, I had no idea that tens of thousands of people would sign up to receive it. After about a year of writing it, I realised I'd landed on a good idea. It was at that point I decided I wanted to try and make money from my newsletter. So, I sat down and wrote a business plan. I spent hours researching different ways I could monetise the newsletter until I figured out a model that I thought would work. My newsletter now brings in the equivalent of a full-time salary for two days' work a week.

The reason I'm able to make money from my newsletter isn't because I know some magic business secrets (I pretty much Googled everything I needed!). It's because I *believed* it was possible to make money from a creative project and I took the necessary steps to action that belief. The idea was an accident; the money wasn't.

How we think about money affects how we make money. We all have beliefs about money, which either help or hinder our abilities to earn more of it. Our surroundings shape these beliefs – from how we were raised and what we were taught at school, to media portrayals of wealth and poverty. None of this is to deny that socioeconomic structures make it harder for some to reach their earning potential than others but I do believe we can improve our personal financial circumstances to an impactful extent. Put simply, in order to start feeling more comfortable talking about money, first you have to unpack the beliefs you hold about it.

Go through the following list of commonly held beliefs and tick off which ones you identify with.

- Money is evil
- Money doesn't buy happiness

- I'm not the sort of person who can earn a lot of money
- Money means freedom
- Money can help people
- If I make money, I will turn into a bad person
- I have no control over how much money I can make
- I can't make money and be happy
- I have to work hard to make money
- It's impolite to talk about money in public
- Telling people how much I earn is boasting

Now you have an idea about your beliefs, you can dig into how they affect your business of one. Perhaps you've held back from charging higher rates because you don't believe you're the sort of person who can earn a lot of money. Or maybe you think it's boastful to talk about how much you earn, so you shy away from asking freelance friends to share their rates with you.

As for how to overcome limiting beliefs – you challenge them. Ask yourself a simple question: is this belief actually based in fact, or is it just that – a belief? Try it next time you're facing an uncomfortable money challenge, like a fee negotiation. As those familiar feelings of discomfort, shame or guilt come up, take a step back from the situation and work out how a limiting belief might be impacting your thought patterns and reactions.

Money shame

Do you ever worry about being a sell-out? I do.

When I started out as a journalist over ten years ago, ire was thrown at anyone who did a bit of copywriting on the side. When I worked at a media organisation in a sponsored content team, there was an 'us and them' atmosphere between my department and the newsroom. In short, if you did anything other 'pure journalism', you were a sell-out.

After I went freelance, however, I quickly realised that all this kind of thinking did was make me feel guilty about my income. The accusation of selling out feeds a dangerous idea that success is scarce and needs to be hoarded. While strides have been made in the last few years to move away from these outdated notions of selling out, judgemental perceptions about how creatives should make their money nonetheless prevail.

Being perceived as a sell-out is a creative's worst nightmare; as such, worry that such criticism may be levied at you sits beneath the surface of every business decision you make. Even though I know that the reality of high London living costs and poor freelance journalism rates means that I have to do commercial work, that doesn't stop me feeling weird about it. I regularly do a sweep of my bylines to make sure I've written 'enough' articles for mainstream newspapers recently to justify my status as a journalist.

Selling out is as problematic a term as it's always been. Especially when we talk about female creatives because when you say a woman is a sell-out, what you're really saying is that she's 'done enough now'. And it's time we put the loaded and judgemental phrase to bed. It's not surprising that so many see commercial work as 'selling out', as I believe that these thoughts stem from a type of shame. We are all affected by 'money shame' in some way, whether that's because we feel the need to justify the source of our income, are uncomfortable talking about money or have experienced debt ourselves.

If the thought of talking about money makes you feel uncomfortable, you may not be enjoying reading this chapter right now. If that's the case, have you ever stopped to ask yourself *why* you feel so uncomfortable talking about money? Perhaps someone told you talking about money was impolite, maybe you have a negative image of rich people or maybe you disagree with the mechanisms of late capitalism. I challenge you to work out exactly what it is about money that makes you feel so awkward around it.

After working mum Clare Seal reached breaking point with her debt, she started an anonymous Instagram account to document her journey out of it. In her book about her relationship with money, *Real Life Money: An honest guide to taking control of your finances*, she explains the shame she felt for being in debt. 'The stigma of debt and financial difficulty provides precisely the right conditions ... for shame to thrive and grow: secrecy, silence and judgement.' Being in debt is of course a common source of shame. Other sources are growing up without money; growing up *with* money; parents or a partner financially supporting you; spending all of your inheritance in one go; not earning enough money; or earning a lot of money. The list goes on.

Looking at that list, you probably have a sense of where your money shame comes from but do you know *why* you feel so ashamed? We all tell ourselves stories about money and our relationship to it but it's important to map out exactly where that narrative comes from. A simple exercise to help do that is to write out your money story. Start with your earliest memory of money, which might be something like a parent giving you a piggy bank or not being able to buy you the Christmas gift you asked for. From there, work your way through your life up to the present moment detailing the moments when money came up, how it was talked about and what your feelings around it were.

This exercise will help you see what patterns emerge for you around money and it might help you make sense of why you feel a certain way about it. For example, if you grew up in a household where money was considered an impolite topic of conversation, it might help you explain why, when you found yourself in debt in your early twenties, you were unable to ask anyone for help.

The thing about shame is that once you name it, it starts to shrink.

Find people to talk about money with

I'm in a WhatsApp group set up with the sole purpose of talking candidly about money. The most common message posted is someone asking to be bolstered as they go into a salary or fee negotiation. When one of these requests comes through, my phone comes alive with the buzz of a dozen messages of encouragement supporting the person.

A 2018 study from the bank Starling found that people gained more financial confidence from discussing money than from putting it away in their savings accounts. In her book *Open Up: The power of talking about money*, the author Alex Holder advocates the hosting of 'money salons'. A money salon is a meetup with friends with the express purpose of talking about money.

'Start talking about money and I promise everyone will follow. Something happens when this topic is opened. Once the tension is released people can't stop themselves from joining in.

They might not share exact salaries or figures in their bank account but people will reveal spending plans, revelatory moments and a bit of entertaining gossip on mutual friends.'

Topics Holder suggests starting with: student loans, who can afford to buy a flat and exes' spending habits. Once you've built up courage, move on to the harder topics of paying off debts, what your parents taught you about money, whether you budget and your ultimate money goals.

You might feel like you have no one to talk about money with but if you seek out the right spaces you'll be surprised. Maybe you have a friend in your circle you're close enough to open this dialogue with. Get in the habit of normalising money conversations. Ask freelance colleagues for their rates, talk about money with your friends. How we feel about discussing money is influenced by many factors, including our upbringing, culture and gender. For anyone who doesn't feel comfortable talking about money, know that this doesn't have to be a fixed state. You can practise until you are OK having these conversations by finding others to talk to regularly.

It's vital to have spaces where you can get comfortable having messy money conversations, as they are a practice ground for when you need to have a difficult money discussion in a more formal setting.

Putting Your Money Where Your Mouth Is

I've talked about talking about money, now it's time to actually talk figures. In the following pages, I'm going to share practical advice on how to set your rates and ask for more money.

How to set your prices

When it comes to setting a price, the good news is that there's a cold, hard science to it. According to Peter Hill, chartered accountant and business growth specialist, pricing should be an unemotional act – 'simply another business skill to be learned, developed and implemented in your business'.

In his book *Pricing for Profit*, he outlines how most businesses, both large and small, avoid action on pricing because they don't know anything about the subject. They don't assess their pricing out of fear. You can change all that by learning some simple maths and understanding the different ways to set a price.

There are dozens of pricing strategies, ranging from psychological pricing (supermarkets charging £9.99 rather than £10) and pay-what-you-can (museums asking for a suggested donation), to price skimming (electronics companies initially setting a high price for their computers and then bringing it down as newer models come out). I want to keep this book a jargon-free zone so I won't go into arduous detail about pricing strategies. Instead, here I've briefly outlined the main strategies that are most applicable to those who work for themselves. I think it's important to lay these strategies out because there are methods behind them. Understanding different pricing models and how some are more appropriate depending on your industry and business helps to remove the emotion from thinking about pricing.

It's very likely that you're already using one or more of the most common types of pricing strategies without even being aware of it.

Hourly pricing

An hourly pricing strategy is simply the exchange of time for money. It involves selling your time to a client in hourly slots or on a day rate. The majority of service-based freelancers use an hourly (or daily) pricing strategy. It works best when the work is simple and repetitive, such as administrative work. See 'Time isn't money' on page 87 for why this model isn't always the best approach.

Project-based pricing

Project-based pricing involves setting a flat fee for your work. You can determine the fee based on the estimated time it will take you to complete the work or you can set the price based on the value of the deliverables. Like the hourly pricing strategy, charging by the project works well for service-based freelancers, particularly highly skilled and in-demand creatives.

Value-based pricing

Value-based pricing is set according to the customer or client's perceived value of your product or service. It's based on the assumption that customers and clients will pay more for something if they believe it to be of significant value to them. Value-based pricing works best when you know your clients and customers well and have the data to support your prices. For example, a freelance web designer might use value-based pricing to charge £20,000 to design a website if they can show their client how sales will increase as a direct result of their work.

Freemium pricing

The freemium pricing model offers part of your product for free. If you use a streaming service like Spotify, you're using a freemium product. However, it also has applications for freelancers; my newsletter is a freemium model. This model works best for digital products and ecommerce because the costs of production are minimal. It's good for content creators like podcasters, photographers and writers. A freemium pricing strategy can also be as simple as using social media as a shop window, sharing some of your work for free with the aim of enticing paying clients.

Premium pricing

Premium, or prestige, pricing is used for selling luxury goods and services. You set an artificially high price to reflect how your product or service is top end. Premium pricing is often exclusive. It's based on the idea that some clients and customers want a product that isn't affordable to everyone.

This pricing strategy works well for businesses with a strong brand identity. Your business needs a reputation for quality and/or status. Any type of business can use premium pricing, from service-based businesses like coaches, consultants and stylists, to artisans making products.

Cost-plus pricing

The cost-plus strategy uses the cost of producing your product or service to determine your price. You start with how much it costs you to make your product and then you mark up the price. For example, a freelance florist buys flowers for £10 and wants to make a profit of £5 per arrangement so charges £15, giving them a mark-up of 50%. Cost-plus pricing is best for the sale of physical goods because these items have associated production costs. Anything that involves raw materials, from jewellery and carpentry to floristry and prints, can be priced using this strategy.

Competition-based pricing

Competition-based pricing, or competitive pricing, uses the going market rate to set a price for your good or service. This strategy uses what your competitors are charging as a benchmark. When you use a competition-based pricing strategy you will set a price either slightly higher or slightly lower than your direct competition, based on how you want to position yourself in relation to your competitor. This works best if you sell something that doesn't have a tangible cost of production, such as digital products or events.

Time isn't money

A typical trajectory for many freelancers is to start out by charging by the hour (or day). In effect, this is a straightforward exchange of time for money. The good thing about the hourly pricing strategy is that it's simple – both for you as the freelancer to account for and for the client to understand. However, the downside of charging by the hour is that it leaves you vulnerable to falling into what's known as the 'freelance trap'. In *Open Up*, Alex Holder talks about the perils of this: the thought that all your time is a potential opportunity to earn money. 'There is a danger with freelancing to never say no to work and to start judging time against how much you could earn, a trip to see your mum = £200, a hangover = £150, going to your kid's sports day = £350. But this is no way to live.'

Hourly pricing works best when the work you're doing takes a predictable amount of time, for example, bookkeeping, data inputting and even personal services. It's possible to accurately estimate how long this work will take, whereas writing a report, creating a strategy or designing a logo is more subjective. I've also found that when I price by the hour for this kind of work, it assumes that my time is always worth the same amount. So, if a client hires me for one project at an hourly rate and then asks me to do more complex work, they expect the price to stay the same. Now my rule of thumb is that whenever there's thinking time involved in a project, I don't price by the hour but by the project instead. As for determining that rate, I base it on my value – a concept that took me a long time to get my head around but ultimately helped me understand what it means to charge what I'm actually worth.

Value is what makes something desirable. The futurist Max Borders wrote how time, perspective and context all influence our individual perceptions of value. He used the example of a man doing his laundry in a hurry who finds himself short a quarter. The man's in a real bind as he needs to dry his trousers for a dinner that night. Then another guy comes in with a big bag of quarters. The first man asks if he can buy a quarter from him for a dollar. 'At that time, in that context, from my perspective, his quarter was worth at least a dollar to me,' Borders writes.

I take a lot of comfort from this story because it high-lights the subjective nature of value. Not even a quarter – a unit of money – always holds the same value to two different people. I find this concept liberating because it means that how much someone wants to pay for my work isn't about me at all. It's about the time, context and perspective of the other person – subjective things I can't do a whole lot about. I could've walked into that laundry room on a different day, trying to sell a quarter for a dollar, and been laughed at. But if I happen upon a panicked man with sopping wet trousers, I'm up 75 cents.

Your value as a freelancer is made up of your skills, expertise and creativity. How much you can charge for those things depends on how desirable they are to your buyer. I once had a conversation with a freelance friend about how much to charge for speaking at a virtual event. We were discussing whether to charge less because the event wasn't held in person, the logic being that ticket prices were lower and there was no travel time involved. The line of thinking seemed sound enough – if the event is making less money, surely as a speaker, I should charge less, too. Except that's not the best way to measure your value. Whether an event is held virtually or in person doesn't have any bearing on the price you, as the speaker, can charge.

Think about it this way – what's my value as a speaker at that online event? Well, to start with, I've been asked to deliver this talk because I'm in possession of something valu-able to the event organisers and the audience will buy tickets because of it. That value is agnostic of whether or not I have to travel to deliver the talk. If anything, my ability to deliver a compelling talk over Zoom, which arguably requires even more energy than an in-person talk, holds its own unique value. The key here is understanding that costs – both yours and the clients' – don't factor into the value equation. Let's reverse the example to make that clearer. Let's say you as the speaker are based in London, paying hefty rent for your live/ work loft space. If you base how much you charge the event organiser for your talk on your costs, you'd factor in your high rent and charge a premium. Well, what happens if you move out of the metropolis and your rent drops – do you charge less? Absolutely not.

Pricing is a process. You might start with one pricing strategy and then find that it needs tweaking or that your business develops and a different strategy becomes more appropriate. You might also mix and match strategies. As long as you've developed some strategy for pricing, however you decide to price is fine. Move away from charging by the hour by learning about pricing strategies, find people to practise talking about money with and charge what you're actually worth, not what someone else thinks they can get away with. Don't fall into the freelance trap.

How I use different pricing strategies in my freelancing business

Let's pull all of this together by taking a look at some of the different pricing strategies going on in the different areas of my own freelancing business.

- I send out one free newsletter a week and the readers who pay a monthly fee receive additional benefits and perks. This is a freemium pricing model because the portion of readers who pay make the entire publication possible.

- I'm paid per article when I write for newspapers and magazines. This is project-based pricing because I charge a flat fee which is based on a combination of the value of my work and the time it takes me to complete it.
- When corporate clients ask me for consulting services, I charge them a day rate. I exchange my time for money, making this an hourly pricing strategy.
- I sell tickets for the panel events and workshops I run for freelancers. I determine the price of these tickets based on what other event organisers charge for similar events. If there's another event happening around the same time as mine, I might choose to price mine slightly lower to encourage people to attend it. This is competitive pricing because I'm using the market rate as a benchmark for my own prices.
- My podcast makes money through advertising. This is value-based pricing because we set a price according to the perceived value the advertiser will get, which in this case is positive brand association.

You don't need to get lost in the weeds of pricing strategies. For the most part, I don't agonise over whether to use an hourly or project-based strategy when I'm setting my rate for a piece of work. Instead I just make sure that I've priced something based on its value to the client or customer and presented it in a way they will understand.

There are also many occasions when you don't have any say in how your work is priced. For example, the work I do in the publishing and media industries is paid according to industry standards with little room for negotiation. But for when you can set your rates, what I've laid out here is intended to help you to start to think strategically about how to do so. By understanding the methods behind pricing you will be able to remove the emotion from it and see it as simply a normal part of doing business.

How to use pricing strategies as a freelancer

According to Peter Hill, the accountant and pricing expert, value-based pricing is the best pricing strategy. 'The only true way to set your selling prices is through value pricing, which is establishing a value to each of your products for each of your customers and then pricing them accordingly.'

The huge advantage freelancers have over larger businesses is that many of them can set a different price for individual clients. However, many freelancers are so scared of a negative reaction from their customers and clients that their default is to set their prices too low from the outset.

When I spoke to Hill about how freelancers can use value-based pricing strategies in their businesses of one, he told me a pricing strategy hack is for the freelancer to assess the cost of the client *not* hiring them. For example, if a company does not hire a freelance web designer then they will have to create their own website. This is likely to result in wordy copy, user-unfriendly design and ultimately a loss of sales. 'A freelancer has to think through the process of a client not buying from them. That will help them get to the value of that mistake,' Hill said.

Hill emphasised the importance of determining the value of what you do as the starting point of determining your price. A simple way to do this is by asking your client or customer a critical question before you set your price with them: *What do you want and how quickly do you want it?*

Knowing this will help you understand what problem your client or customer needs solving and therefore what value you will provide through your work. For example, a client might need a floral arrangement urgently, in which case it's no good trying to sell them an exotic flower with a long lead time but you can charge them a premium for next-day delivery of a classic arrangement. The same principle holds true for a freelance graphic designer whose client wants a brand redesign – you can sell them a package that includes a bespoke typeface because the value to them is standing out from their competitors.

When it comes to value, another stumbling block for freelancers is the fact they work from home and therefore feel uncomfortable charging a premium. Hill told me this is an issue he sees time and again. 'Many freelancers value their time based on the "cost" of their time, usually worked out from a calculation of "I want to earn £X so need to charge £Y per hour",' he said. 'Instead, freelancers need to ensure they're setting prices based on the *value* of their expertise, skill and creativity. This is not determined by whether you work in central London in expensive offices or from your bedroom.'

You may have heard this story or a variation of it before, but it illustrates a crucial point:

A business has a huge machine that stops working. Every hour it's down costs the business £10,000 in lost revenue. They try everything without success but eventually find an expert they fly in from abroad. She spends 20 minutes inspecting the machine and then hits it with a hammer. It springs back to life. She sends a bill for £30,000 which the company challenges as she was only there for 20 minutes, and even with travel time and costs that comes to nowhere near £30,000. Her response? 'It only took me 20 minutes, but it took 40 years to know where to hit the machine.'

How to negotiate a rate

When I was a newbie reporter early on in my career, I was assigned a story to write tips to help people start a new job on the right foot. In researching the story, I came across a fascinating 2007 study from MIT and UC Berkeley about salary negotiation. The researchers found that how employees perceived the negotiation mattered more to them than how much money they got. It didn't actually matter whether a person got the money they'd asked for but just the fact they'd asked for it gave them a feeling of self-worth and confidence.

This tidbit has stuck with me ever since. It doesn't matter what they say but it will matter to you that you asked. Now, I negotiate every offer I'm made. The only exception to this is when the offer exceeds my expectations. In order to have an expectation, however, you need to have a figure in mind before you go into any rate negotiation.

Well, you actually need *two* figures before you go into a negotiation – the lowest amount you'd be willing to accept for this work and what you'd ideally like to be paid for it. Neither of these figures should be plucked out of thin air. The range you set should be based on a well-researched pricing strategy, using one of the techniques outlined earlier. At the very least, ask around your freelance friends to find out what you can expect to get paid for this type of work.

Assuming the figure given to you doesn't exceed your expectations, you then start the negotiation. When it comes to asking for more money, you always need to justify it. 'I just think I'm worth more than this' may very well be true, but you need to give the client a reason *they* feel is objective.

Here are some examples of objective reasons to ask for a higher fee:

- This project needs to be completed urgently. In order for me to complete it by the deadline I need to charge a premium.
- I have valuable access to a client, network or material which is superior to what my competitors can offer.
- The work that's required will take more time than has been accounted for in the project brief.
- My other clients pay more for this kind of work.

Another negotiating technique is the 'tip clause'. This involves offering the client the chance to pay you a 'tip' after you deliver the work. For example, say you're asked to do a piece of work by a new client you've not worked with before, which you believe is worth £2,000 but they've said their budget is £1,000. Go back to them and say you'll accept their offer but that you'd like them to 'tip' you once they see how good your work is. You say something along the following lines: 'I believe the value of my work for this project is £2,000 and that once I've delivered it you will agree! However, I appreciate it's hard to judge that without seeing it so I propose to set a minimum fee of £1,000 and leave the payment of any balance to your discretion, at any level from £1,000 to £3,000.'

If there's no room for a price increase, or if it doesn't meet your minimum amount, don't panic! You do have other options. The first is to reduce the scope of the work. Propose a lighter version of the project they're asking for that will take you less time. So, rather than lower your rate, keep it the same but make the project smaller.

For example, if you're a journalist and you're negotiating the price of a feature that would require three interviews and expert commentary, counter-offer a one-interview Q&A. If you're a PR strategist and you're negotiating a two-day workshop and strategy document, counter-offer a two-hour phone call and one-page strategy document. If you're a caterer and you're negotiating a wedding package, counter-offer less expensive starters or fewer canapes.

You can also negotiate non-monetary items. Will they cover expenses? Can you ask for half the fee upfront? Does the company make a product they could give you as a freebie or discounted perk? (NB: I mean *perk*, not in lieu of compensation.)

If you really can't get your minimum price, you need to make a call about whether or not to accept the work anyway. There will be instances in which accepting a lower price will be in your interest.

This is where I use what I call the golden triangle of free-lance work. The golden triangle of freelance work is when a project is fun, pays well and looks good. It's fun in the sense that you actually enjoy the work – you either find the scope interesting or you enjoy working with the particular client. It pays well in terms of the raw figure but also the client pays on time and without any fuss. And it looks good, in the sense that the client has gravitas in your field so working for them will either raise your profile or land you more work.

If you do decide to accept a lower rate, be intentional about it. It's fine to accept lower rates every now and again but consistently undervaluing yourself and your work only erodes your self-esteem and also brings the overall wages down for everyone else.

Here's an email template you can use to send to a client if their initial offer doesn't meet your expectations. Use the suggested reasons as a guide for explaining why your work is worth more than their offer.

> Hi New Client,
> Thank you for sending this over. The project looks brilliant and I'm excited to get started. Re: the fee, for this kind of project, I typically charge £XX. This is because [I charge a premium for expediating projects with such a tight deadline/I have exclusive access to material that you won't find anywhere else/based on my experience, this project will take longer than outlined and I need to account for the extra time].
> Looking forward to working with you.
> Thanks,
> Anna

How to negotiate a rate when you don't know the market

What about when you're negotiating a rate for work you've never done before?

It happens all the time. You might be new to freelancing or working in a field in which you don't have much previous experience. For example, I'm a trained journalist and when I started freelancing, I was asked to do some consulting work for a PR company. I could do the work, no problem, but I didn't know what to charge. When the client asked, 'What's your rate?' I had no idea what to say.

The former FBI negotiator Chris Voss recommends getting around this issue by letting the other party make the first offer. In his book *Never Split the Difference: Negotiating as if your life depended on it*, he suggests 'letting the other side anchor monetary negotiations'. In other words, let them make the first move.

As Voss writes, 'The real issue is that neither side has perfect information going to the table. This often means you don't know enough to open with confidence. That's especially true anytime you don't know the market value of what you are buying or selling.'

By letting your client go first, you can get a sense of what's a reasonable rate. So many freelancers avoid negotiating for the simple reason that they're afraid of looking stupid. No one wants to ask for a figure that's way too high or too low. By asking them to go first, you dodge that problem. You might also get lucky – they might offer a figure that's higher than the top of your range.

So how do you actually bat the question back to the client? Simple:

Client: What's your rate?

You: It would be great if you could share what your budget is for this project so that I can put together a tailored proposal.

Chapter Summary: Talking about Money

If you learn how to get comfortable talking about money, you'll be better equipped to look after your financial health, build your wealth and advocate for yourself – plus your business of one will flourish as a result!

Cultivate a millionaire's mindset: No one gets rich, or makes money in their business, by accident. Most millionaires accumulate their wealth by living within their means, spending a lot of time budgeting and making careful financial decisions. It's within anyone's grasp to practise these healthy money habits.

Challenge money taboos: Our own limiting beliefs – born out of our upbringing and social taboos – hold us back from earning what we deserve. Challenge your personal money gremlins by working out what it is about money that you find shameful and find people with whom you can openly talk about financial matters.

Understand the fundamentals of pricing: Take the emotion out of pricing by learning the basics of pricing strategies. Establish the value you provide to your customers or clients by asking one crucial question: *What do you want and how quickly do you want it?* Once you understand how they perceive the value of your product or service, price accordingly.

Negotiate like a pro: The secret to negotiating is to go into it knowing what you want to get out of it. If the offer doesn't meet your expectation, then you give the client an *objective reason* for asking for more money. If you're asked for your rate and you don't know what to say, ask the client to give their figure first.

FREELANCER STORY

Kristabel Plummer (@iamkristabel) – online content creator

I started my blog, I Want You to Know, around 12 years ago while I was a student and went full-time freelance as a content creator in 2014. I'd wanted to be a fashion designer with my own label but became disillusioned after I started working for a high street brand and I didn't like some of their unethical practices. So, I thought that I'd run my own project but make it a blog; instead of making a product, I make content. I channel the ethos of what I imagined my label to be into my work, something that's inclusive and colourful.

When I first started out, I won an award which came as a big shock at the time. I had so much imposter syndrome about it and thought they'd made a mistake picking me. I look back now and think it's funny how there are plenty of people who get things that they haven't earned, and there I was doubting an accolade. There's a lot of self-doubt, especially when you do something completely new, which is tied up with how you feel about yourself. It's still an ongoing journey unpacking all that. One of the ways I dealt with feelings of self-doubt and loneliness was by joining a

---

co-working space. It really helped with seeing that I'm not alone in feeling alone, overwhelmed and a bit fed up at times. Working for yourself feels like a constant experiment. You don't have to get up and start at nine every day but it can be a challenge to unlearn the things that perhaps weren't serving us in the first place. You might want to build in something like an annual review but maybe with someone else who's freelance and on your own schedule. For me, learning boundaries has been very important. I now have a permanent out-of-office on emails to set the expectation of when someone will hear back from me. Even if they don't read it, I know I've made my position clear.

Working in a new and growing industry like content creation and influencing is exciting and overwhelming at the same time. There are so many opportunities and anything is possible but you can be your own worst enemy. It's good to have a support network but you've got to build that for yourself because there's no HR team to do it. It was redesigning my blog that really helped me figure out what I wanted to do with my career. I hired a graphic designer to redo my site and she sent me a questionnaire asking me what I wanted to communicate with my business. That was the first time I thought about why I was doing this and how it was because I'd felt so alienated by traditional media. I said, OK, this is me, a Black woman talking about knitting, fashion, putting different colours together while living in London and finding time to travel. That's how I really figured out what I stood for.

CHAPTER FIVE

Funding Your Freelancing

When I worked for other people, making money was straight-forward. A company would hire me to work for them in exchange for a fixed salary, paid into my bank account on a monthly basis. The company's financial health wasn't reflected in my pay cheque. If the commercial department landed a lucrative new contract, I didn't get more money that month, nor did a missed sales target result in a pay cut for me. Even if any of these things were going on, I was none the wiser because I had no clue what was happening under the bonnet of any of the companies I used to work at. I had no idea how they were making their money.

I understood the big picture, sure. When I worked for news-papers, I knew they made money by selling copies of the paper, through advertising and a few other tangential commercial ventures. But the finer details of their business model were a mystery to me. How much money was made from newspaper sales compared to the revenue digital advertising brought in? What other revenue streams did the company have? How much money was in the bank should a financial disaster strike? For the most part, there wasn't a whole lot I could do to learn this information; it was kept private from the employees. Just like you're not 'supposed to' ask how much someone earns, seem-ingly you can't ask your boss how much the company made that quarter.

On the rare occasions when the company executives trotted out some charts and graphs at the end of the financial year, I didn't really understand what they demonstrated. I have an economics A-level and learned about economies of scale and price elasticity of demand but the basics of how a business is run were kept out of the classroom. When I started working for myself, I found myself in the deep end. I realised that if I didn't learn a few basic business principles, my freelancing plans were destined to sink. Put simply, if you want to work for yourself, you need to understand how you can actually make money from it.

To my surprise, I found I really enjoyed learning this stuff. Gone are the days when understanding how a business works means paying vast sums of money for an expensive degree or poring over hefty textbooks. I learned from other freelancers and business-of-one owners. I asked people, 'How did you actually do that?' I read books and listened to podcasts by people who run the types of businesses I'm interested in. So I am now going to show you that the business side of working for yourself doesn't have to be boring. It can be a place for curiosity, experimentation and creativity.

In this chapter, you'll learn:

- How you can make money working for yourself
- A simple template for writing a business plan
- Seven income streams for freelancers

How Do I Actually Make Money for Myself?

Let's go back to basics and address a fundamental question that anyone who wants to work alone needs to understand.

How does somebody make money when they work for themselves? The simple answer is: they sell a product or service to a customer or client.

For example, a freelance writer sells the service of writing articles to their clients, magazine editors. A freelance illustrator sells the product of a print to their customers, art lovers. They cover the costs of producing that good or service. These costs can include raw materials as well as the time it takes to make the item. A freelance writer's costs will be the time it takes them to write their article, while an illustrator's costs will also include the pens and paper they need to buy to make their artwork. They then collect the fee for their good or service. This process can happen at the point of sale or afterwards, in some cases even up to 120 days later. The illustrator might charge the full fee for the print upfront, whereas the freelance writer might only get paid after the article is published.

The business makes a profit if the amount left over after the total costs are deducted from the amount made from sales is a positive number. For example, an illustrator charges £200 for a print. Her costs are £100 in materials. That leaves her with £100 profit. From that profit, she then has to pay tax. Whatever is left over is money in her pocket, which she can either reinvest in her business, perhaps to buy more materials, or she can pay herself.

This lesson in freelancer economics might seem obvious but it's important to go back to basics and get really clear on how our businesses actually work. These fundamentals give you a good foundation for mastering more complex concepts, like business plans, loans and revenue streams. In this chapter, I'm going to cover the different ways you can fund a freelance business, from how to structure your revenue streams to the different external financing options available to you.

Write a business plan the easy way

You don't need a business plan but you do need a plan for your business.

When you hear the term *business plan*, your mind probably conjures up an image of a man in an ill-fitting suit delivering a dull presentation on a flipchart in a stuffy conference room. Like all business jargon, it sounds more complicated – and often more boring – than it really needs to be. In reality, a business plan is just a document that contains important information about your business idea. It's supposed to help you clarify an idea, identify any potential issues and set your goals.

What often ends up happening, however, is that the plan gets written and then forgotten about. Most people only write business plans when they need to, for example when they're seeking a loan. That doesn't mean you don't need a business plan at all, rather that you need a straightforward one that you'll actually use.

A traditional business plan is a lengthy document, spanning dozens of pages. A much simpler framework you can use in place of a business plan is the Business Model Canvas. Developed by Alex Osterwalder, co-founder of software company Strategyzer, this is used by businesses of any size the world over to map out an idea and turn it into a plan of action. It was designed using the principle that there are nine building blocks all successful businesses need:

1. A value proposition – *What value do you provide your clients or customers? What problems do you solve for people?*
2. Customer segments – *Who are your different customers?*
3. Channels – *How are you reaching your customers?*
4. Customer relationships – *How do you get, keep and grow your customers?*
5. Revenue streams – *How will you make money?*
6. Key resources – *What resources do you need to deliver your value proposition?*
7. Key partners – *What suppliers, contractors and vendors do you need to work with?*
8. Key activities – *What are you going to do?*
9. Cost structure – *What costs do you have?*

By laying out these blocks in a grid system, you get a bird's eye view of your business idea – you can see exactly what you're offering to whom and how you're going to make money from it. You can use the BMC to plot a brand-new idea or you can use it to fine-tune an existing one. You can download a template from www.strategyzer.com. If you don't like this format, you can still use the prompts and questions above to outline your vision in a way that makes sense to you.

The most important thing is that when you put together a business plan for the first time, you do it in a way that's actually going to get you excited. If your job involves writing, think of your business plan more like a story – write it out like you would any other narrative. If you work better using visuals, draw the plan. As you'll see later in this chapter, there are circumstances in which you need to show your business plan to third parties but worry about that part later. For now, just get it on the page.

Seven Income Streams for Freelancers

You might have heard the saying that the average millionaire has seven streams of income. Numerous studies have shown that the way to accumulate wealth is through having different sources of revenue. Millionaires who work a demanding day job supplement their income through investments, be that in the stock market, by investing in other people's businesses or through a property portfolio. Multiple income streams, however, aren't just for the super-rich. They make good financial sense for everyone.

Over the last two decades, we've seen the dotcom bubble burst, the global financial market go into a severe recession and the socioeconomic fallout of a pandemic. The only thing that's certain at this point is uncertainty. In response, a mantra I've come to live by is *don't put your all eggs in one basket.*

First and foremost, diversifying your income helps you reduce your risk. The more ways you have to make money, the more your risk is spread out. This is especially important because we find ourselves in a time in which entire industries are collapsing overnight. Having a second, third or even fourth revenue stream to fall back on is vital.

Secondly, to put it bluntly, additional revenue streams can help you make more money. As a freelancer, there's only one of you and, eventually, you'll hit a ceiling of how much of your time you can trade for money. Some revenue streams enable you to scale your business and significantly grow your income without you needing to start working weekends.

Another great reason to start an additional revenue stream is simply for the joy of working on a new project. As you'll see later on in this chapter, one of my revenue streams is a podcast that I co-host with my best friend, the writer and business coach Tiffany Philippou. While that project makes some money, it's a modest income and it's not the reason why we do it. Getting to work with a friend on a creative project that's a challenge for us has flexed a new business skill but also enriched our friendship.

Whether it's pandemics, tech disruptions or political upheaval, we need to get used to rapid change and be prepared to weather economic uncertainty. The biggest asset you have as a freelancer is your agility, so use it now to adapt to the new normal. With all that in mind, here are my seven income streams for freelancers and businesses of one:

1. Services

If you want to make money working for yourself, services are the best place to start. Packaging up your skills, creativity and expertise into something that another person can buy from you is the foundation of any successful service-based business. The great thing about services is that the sky's the limit with what you can turn into one. When you boil it down, a service is making or doing something for someone else.

Developing a new service business starts with asking yourself the question: what are you good at that you also enjoy doing? From there, you start to sketch out how you can do this skill for someone else. Here are some common freelance services to get you started with some ideas:

- Content creation (writing, photography, illustrating, audio, video, design)
- Lifestyle services (hairdressing, makeup, personal styling, personal training)
- Professional services (bookkeeping, accounting, business coaching, business support)
- Tech services (website designing, data analysis)
- Marketing and sales services (PR, copywriting, social media marketing)
- Event services (party planning, catering, lighting, design)

2. Products

Products can be either physical or digital and they can be sold either directly or indirectly. For example, an illustrator could sell physical prints directly from their website or a writer could sell books indirectly through a publisher. You can also sell things like e-books and digital downloads from your own website.

If your main income stream is a service, think about how you can 'productify' it. A successful freelancer I know is often asked to deliver talks and workshops on how to build a personal brand. She used that skill and knowledge to create a downloadable PDF for people to do the exercises in their own time, which she sells directly from her website.

You can also sell other people's products for a percentage of the profit. This is something freelance hairdressers do frequently, selling hair products alongside their hair styling services. If you already have a product, you can reverse the process and create a complementary service. The London-based studio Kana's main product is its line of handmade ceramics but they also use their studio space for pottery workshops and events.

3. Subscriptions

A subscription model is when your customers pay to receive a product or service on a regular basis. When you think of subscription services, companies like Netflix, Spotify and Hello Fresh come to mind, but you don't have to be a tech giant to develop a successful membership-based revenue stream. For online creators, platforms like Patreon, Substack and YouTube Membership enable you to create a subscription option for your existing followers. Anyone with an engaged online following can start a subscription-based service. The keyword there is *engaged* – you don't need tens of thousands of followers to do this but you do need loyal fans.

A subscription model also works for physical products. After all, in the first iteration of Netflix, subscribers paid a monthly fee and received DVDs in the post! For example, the illustrator Natalie Byrne sends her Patreon subscribers one of her postcards with a handwritten note in the post.

Developing an audience-funded model can generate the holy grail of dependable monthly income. I run a subscription-based newsletter and it's my most reliable income. This isn't passive income, though, and you'll spend a lot of your time on admin and marketing. As long as you don't go into this option thinking you can make money in your sleep, it will be worth the effort.

4. F2B and F2C work

You may have heard of the terms B2C and B2B. They stand for business-to-consumer and business-to-business, respectively. Business-to-consumer is the process of selling directly to consumers who are also the end users of your product or service. Amazon, Starbucks and Netflix are all B2C businesses. B2B, on the other hand, involves selling to another business. WeWork, Xerox and Slack all sell their products to other businesses, as do wholesale manufacturers. It's important to understand the distinction between these business models because they also exist in the freelance space. I like to think of them as F2C and F2B.

You work out whether you're an F2C or F2B freelancer by asking yourself whether the person you're selling your product or service to is the same person who ends up using it. The majority of freelancers operate an F2B model and sell

At their core, brand partnerships and affiliate marketing are advertising techniques in a different skin. They're similar to the product placement you see in movies, when a brand pays to put its product in front of an audience. Now, there are strict regulations, as well as ethical considerations, to take into account when taking money from a brand. The Advertising Standards Authority has guidelines available on its website that you need to adhere to. Beyond what the law says, you should never advertise something that doesn't align with your values, that you've never tried yourself or that you wouldn't buy with your own money. When done transparently, by clearly declaring the financial arrangement to the consumer, there isn't anything inherently wrong with this income stream. If you're open-minded, you'll find this income stream can be a really great way to support a creative career.

7. Public speaking

If you want to make additional income, consider talking for a living. Public speaking runs the gamut from giving a keynote at a conference or moderating a panel discussion to hosting webinars or Instagram Lives.

I fell into public speaking when I started running my own events for freelancers. I would host panels. This opened my eyes to a previously unseen world. In addition to running my own events, I now also deliver talks at companies, host panels at festivals and moderate virtual panels. A freelance writer and coach I know makes the backbone of her income through speaking, often getting paid upwards of £5,000 to deliver a keynote or chair a roundtable discussion.

After I got over the initial terror of my first talk, speaking in public became a lot easier. What I've continued to find hard, however, whether I'm talking in person or online, is how draining it can be. Talking takes time and energy – from preparation and travel (although you don't have to worry about that with virtual events) to feeling tired after delivering your talk. As long as you factor in the time around the talk itself, speaking can do wonders for boosting your confidence, profile and income.

Start an additional income stream in two simple steps

By now, you should have a pretty good idea about the different ways you can make money when you work for yourself. Hopefully you're excited to start adding on new income streams and turn your business into a sustainable operation that can thrive in the years to come. If you're wondering about the practicalities of adding a new income stream string to your bow, here's my two-step method to get you going:

1. Do a skills audit

Make a list of all the skills you already have; don't overlook those that you find easiest as they are your most valuable. Some questions you can ask yourself as a prompt for this exercise are:

- What do you love doing?
- What do your friends tell you you're good at?
- What comes very easily to you?

As you're writing your list, be as specific as possible. If your skill is writing, drill down to what types of writing style or formats you're best at. For example, writing how-to guides. Also, mine your soft skills and include them in your audit as well. Things like figuring out how to do things, uncovering hard-to-find information or getting people to help me do something I don't know how to do are all skills!

The benefit of doing a skills audit is that it helps you get super clear on what options are available to you and your existing expertise. It's very easy to look at that list of revenue streams and think that none would work for you but by starting with the know-how you already have, you'll surprise yourself with how many paths are actually open to you.

2. Pick a stream

Once you've done your skills audit, it's time to pick an income stream from the list on the previous pages. Use the skills you identified in your audit to guide you but also listen to your instinct and go for whichever one jumps out at you.

Don't overthink this step. Just go for the one that gets you most excited, the one that you read and thought, 'I want to do this!' The idea here is to start with what comes easiest and most naturally to you. As you grow your business, your confidence will grow alongside it. You might revisit this exercise in six months or a year's time and find that an income stream that seemed too daunting is now the one that seems most exciting to you.

Next, you want to put your skills together with your income stream to specify what this might look like for your business. For example, let's say you're a freelance writer. You identified writing how-to guides, figuring out how to do things and uncovering hard-to-find information as your skills. Now you want to add teaching to the mix. Use your writing skills to put together a one-pager on what you could teach and to whom and then put your research skills to use by identifying potential clients.

Once you've identified your skills and picked your income stream, you're ready to put it into action. Adding an additional revenue stream means launching an offshoot of your existing business. Use the Business Model Canvas I outlined earlier in this chapter to bring your idea to life and refer back to previous chapters for a refresher on how to find your first clients.

How to make multiple income streams work for you

To help you understand what income streams look like in practice, let's take a look at mine. I have six streams of income in my business:

1. **Journalism:** This includes articles I write for magazines and newspapers.
2. **Commercial work:** This is my F2B work, which consists mainly of writing features for tech companies' blogs.
3. **Public speaking:** This includes speaking at other people's events, as well as hosting my own.
4. **Newsletter subscriptions:** I run a newsletter which makes money through reader subscriptions.

5. **Podcast:** My podcast makes money through sponsorship deals.
6. **Books:** I also make money from book sales, like the one you're reading right now!

In an ideal world, these revenue streams would be fairly evenly split as portions of my total income. In practice, however, that's almost impossible to achieve given the different earning potentials of these streams. For example, traditional journalism – selling articles to magazines – will always earn me less than my newsletter subscriptions for the simple reason that I can sell multiple subscriptions in one go but I can only write one article at a time. The way I approach my income streams is with my 'How much can I afford to lose overnight?' rule. You simply ask yourself, if you were to wake up one morning and one of your income streams had vanished, how much could you afford to lose as a total percentage of your income? For me, this is about 30%, so I try to make sure no single source of income makes up more than a third of my earnings. This is by no means an exact science and often I do miss my own targets, but the point is to be aware of the risks of being too reliant on one single source of income.

What If My Job Doesn't Lend Itself to Multiple Income Streams?

Most creative jobs, especially digital ones, lend themselves to creating multiple income streams. In-person, service-based jobs, such as hairdressing, makeup artistry or personal training, might not seem like obvious candidates for growing a multi-income stream business of one. I firmly believe, however, that no matter what your freelance business does, it needs more than one way to make money. This was proven during the height of the pandemic when bricks-and-mortar businesses were forced to shutter. Without an option to make money through other income streams, these types of businesses are extremely vulnerable.

It's nonetheless important to be realistic as income diversification looks very different for these types of businesses. A key place to start is by expanding your client roster. Right now, could you afford to lose 20% of your customers overnight? If the answer is *hell no!* then focus on how you can bring in more clients and spread your risk of losing the ones you already have. From there, assess what complementary income streams you can run alongside your main business. For example, if you work in the beauty industry, can you set up an online shop to sell products? Or could you teach your skills to others? Can you create a blog for your website with content that addresses customers' common questions, which you can monetise using affiliate links? Use the examples I've outlined in the previous pages as a jumping-off point for exploring new income stream ideas.

You can also diversify your income outside that which your business brings in. Remember those millionaires with seven income streams? One of those streams is investing in the stock market and another one is investing in property. There are projects you can take on in your life outside of your business that can bolster your overall finances.

Some jobs are going to be harder to diversify than others. It's important to be realistic about the amount of time you actually have to dedicate to it. You might very well decide that it's not in your interest to start a new revenue stream and you would rather focus your efforts on your existing service. That's a business decision you've proactively made. Just don't use the excuse of thinking you can't diversify simply because you can't see an obvious way to do it.

The three golden rules of multiple income streams

1. **Overestimate the time commitment:** All of the ideas I've laid out in this chapter are simple but that doesn't mean they're easy. Go into the process knowing there's no such thing as an instant money-making hack. The term 'passive income' does the rounds but, in reality, it's impossible to make money by doing nothing so be prepared to dedicate time to growing any additional income stream.

2. **One at a time:** With so many income streams available, it's tempting to try and launch several at once. Launch one additional income stream at a time so you give yourself the necessary time and space to devote to it. Once you're happy with the results that income stream is giving you, *then* you can add another one.

3. **Play the long game:** There's no single income stream you could launch today that will make you rich tomorrow. The idea behind creating income streams is to build a healthy and robust business of one that guards against unforeseen challenges. If you find yourself trying to launch an income stream out of panic, instead you need to do some crisis management in your business. In chapter 11, I talk about how to handle financial problems.

External Funding Options

Some freelance businesses will need external sources of funding either to get them off the ground or to help them grow further down the line. Your idea might need an initial cash injection to get you started – for example, if you need to buy stock or equipment. Or you might reach a point with your business where you need more cash in order to scale it up, either by hiring staff or by investing in marketing.

You've got three options when it comes to external funding: grants, loans and investment. Before I get into these options, first I need to explain an essential piece of financial jargon you need to understand before seeking external funding: the difference between debt and equity financing. In its simplest terms, taking outside finance for your business will always cost you something. This cost is either the interest you need to pay on money you've borrowed (debt), a stake in the ownership of your business (equity) or, in the case of grant applications, your time.

If you take on debt to finance your business, you don't have to give up any part of the ownership in exchange for the loan (unless, of course, you fail to pay it back!). Equity, however, gives you the opportunity to work with an investor who can share their experience and insights and play an active role in growing your business. A grant, on the other hand, doesn't require you to give up a stake in your business, nor does it need to be repaid.

While 'debt' is a scary word in the personal finance world, it's not the case that one of these financing methods is superior to the other. As I will outline below, each of these options offers different potential benefits and many businesses will use a combination of them over their lifespan.

Borrowing

Debt financing is a loan that you secure against your capital. The word 'debt' triggers negative connotations for most people but in the business world taking on debt is a common way to grow a business. It's helpful to think of it like a mortgage, a manageable debt you take on which you know will pay off in the end.

For example, many businesses of one that have high start-up costs will use a small business loan to buy their initial stock. When Jason Curry, founder of the all-in-one platform for solo creatives, Continuum, was building his previous business, he took out a loan. He told me that the loan funded the creation of products and meant he could generate revenue before having to cover the cost of production. However, he cautioned that the timings were tight, with not much time to pay back the loan; he had to sell to customers quickly in order to bring in the income he needed to start servicing the repayments.

When you borrow money, a lender agrees to loan you a lump sum on the condition it is paid back in full according to their terms. Over the course of the loan, you'll typically also pay interest on the amount you borrowed on top of the capital repayment. Before they offer you a loan, lenders will want to see a detailed business plan with your projected sales and profit figures.

If you decide to borrow money to fund your business, there are lots of options available to you, ranging from business overdrafts and government-backed small business loans to asset finance and personal loans from friends and family. Which type of loan is right for your business depends on a number of factors, such as what stage you're at, what assets you have to secure the loan and whether you need a short- or long-term cash injection. An independent financial advisor will be able to run through your options with you. You can find an advisor through a recommendation or you can seek out free advice from the Business Finance Guide (see directory).

Investment

When you take investment in your business, you sell a share of it in exchange for a capital injection. Typically, you can raise larger sums by taking investment compared to a loan. As they own a portion of the business, your investors will have a keen interest in its health and success. Depending on the type of investor arrangement, they can help you shape the strategy and direction of your business and offer mentorship. Investment options include angel investing and venture capital as well as crowdfunding.

In order to secure investment, you'll need a detailed business plan and to find an investor interested in your idea and industry. Whereas lenders are only interested in whether you have the means to secure your loan, an investor also wants to believe that you, the business owner, have what it takes to make your idea a success.

Grants

Non-profits, foundations and even the government and large corporations give small businesses grants to fund their projects and get their ideas off the ground. Given that the money doesn't have to be paid back, it will come as no surprise that grants are highly competitive. Grant application writing is also a skill in itself. Often they are lengthy and filling them out is time consuming. While the funding body doesn't require the money to be paid back, you have to remember that there's always a reason why they're giving out grants. The criteria for obtaining a grant are typically highly specific and you'll need to demonstrate on your application form exactly why your project fits the bill.

Chapter Summary: Funding Your Freelancing

There are many funding options available to you to help you grow your business. If you learn business basics, mastering the more complex concepts is easy.

Keep your business plan simple: When writing your first business plan, it's important to do so in a way that's going to get you excited. Ditch the 50-page document and instead use the Business Model Canvas to create a one-page framework for turning your idea into an actionable plan.

Diversify your income: Multiple revenue streams will help you make more money, secure your business's future and reduce your risk. The seven freelance income streams are products, services, subscriptions, F2B and F2C work, sponsorships, speaking and teaching.

External funding options: You can seek external funding options in the form of loans, investment or grants to start or grow your business. All three will cost you something, be it a stake in your business, interest on a loan or your time to complete an application.

CHAPTER SIX

DIY Marketing

Can you be a freelancer and not be on social media? That feels like the Internet Age version of the question about a tree falling in the woods – if there was no one there to tweet it, did it actually happen?

Since I started working for myself, my relationship with social media has become increasingly complicated. My Instagram feed gradually stopped being a place to share holiday snaps and instead became a live stream of my CV. Twitter, once a place to crack inane jokes about *The Great British Bake Off*, is now mainly a jobs board. On the one hand, it's a modern marvel that I can use free platforms frequented by billions of daily users to showcase my skills, grow my professional network and actually land work. But on the other, learning how to navigate business opportunities out in the open of the internet, under the gaze of exes and former colleagues, is a daunting prospect. Add into the mix the pressure of needing a strong personal brand and suddenly social media feels like an incredibly stressful – and often distracting – place to be for a freelancer.

There are some internet terms that just make me recoil. 'Personal brand' is one of them. But regardless of how any of us feel about personal brands, we all have one. When someone hears your name, the thoughts and emotions that immediately come to mind are your personal brand. To make matters murkier, when you work for yourself, your personal brand and your business brand are inevitably intertwined. As a result, everything becomes marketing as you become a walking advert for what you do. Even if you take the decision to operate your business under a different name or run separate social media accounts for it, it's still *your* business and will always be an extension of who you are.

The way I've reconciled my conflicting feelings about my personal brand is by thinking of it like a hat stand. A central peg on which everything else sits. Call it a guiding principle, a north star or an anchor; it's a solid foundation that holds everything else together. By thinking about my personal brand in this way, I've come to see it has nothing to do with how many followers I have on Instagram or whether or not I have a blue tick on Twitter. Rather, my reliable, sturdy hat stand of a personal brand keeps me focused on what matters to me and my business. This has made the idea of a personal brand less cringey, and I can see the clear value of it in my business.

In 2009, the *New York Times* bestselling author Simon Sinek gave a TED Talk about what sets great leaders apart. He said that the few leaders and organisations that inspire action in people, rather than those that manipulate them, all do so by following the same simple principle. They start with their *why*. Sinek went on to write *Start with Why: How great leaders inspire everyone to take action,* in which he developed his now widely used model, the Golden Circle, to explain this idea. The Golden Circle inverts the usual process of how, why, when, to put **why** at the core.

The Golden Circle was designed with CEOs and large companies in mind but the principles are just as applicable to a freelancer figuring out their purpose. Before you can communicate *what* you do or *how* you do it, you first explain *why* you do it.

All of us have a why, we just might struggle to articulate it. Speaking aloud what drives you, what gets you out of bed in the mornings, is an act of vulnerability. But at the same time, your why is your superpower. It's authentic and can't be forced. It requires you to know yourself and to be honest about who you are at your core. As you start to reflect on your own mission, acknowledge that the process of finding your why isn't an easy one. However, once you voice it, suddenly personal branding becomes not only easy but necessary. Knowing why you're doing something makes everything you do a whole lot easier.

You might be thinking, 'what on earth have golden circles and hat stands got to do with marketing?' Well it's quite simple. If you want to market yourself and your skills, you need to start by being really clear on your purpose, your why. Here's the thing – the only marketing strategy that's guaranteed to bring in work is one that's applied *consistently*. If there's only one thing you take from this chapter, let it be this: the secret to marketing is sticking to your plan. If you want to see results, you have to keep at it, and I've found that the only way I can stick to something is if I have its purpose clear in my mind in the first place. The worst thing you can do with your marketing is the stop-start method. I'm sure you know what I'm talking about because we all do it – you do some marketing when you need it, stop when you don't and then panic when you realise you have no work lined up. That's how I used to approach my marketing.

As I outlined in chapter five, I have six different ways I make money as a freelancer and all six of those income streams need to be marketed. In all six cases, I have in the past let my marketing slip simply because when things were good I forgot about what it was like when they were bad. When the work is stacked up, you can't remember a time when you weren't busy. But here's the thing, if you want to break out of the feast-and-famine of freelancing, you need a way to maintain a steady, manageable stream of work, so that when you're busy, you're not overwhelmed to the point where you can't get anything done and when you're quiet, it's not a deafening silence.

In chapter two, I talked about how to find your first clients; this chapter is all about building a consistent marketing habit that makes use of a toolbox of resources, and will deliver a steady stream of work and bring the clients to you.

In this chapter, you'll learn:

- The difference between marketing and sales
- Effective marketing strategies for businesses of one
- How to write a marketing plan
- The tools you need to execute your marketing

The DIY Marketing Toolkit

Your DIY marketing toolkit is everything you need to promote your freelancing skills and market your freelance business. Use this as your one-stop shop for levelling up your one-person-strong marketing department.

Marketing and sales: same same, but different

Most of us know that marketing and sales are two separate functions within a business. The clue's right there in the fact that large companies have a different department for each. But what exactly is the difference between marketing and sales? An easy way to distinguish the two is by remembering that *marketing comes before sales*. That's to say, marketing is the process of finding the potential customers for your product or service and then sales is the act of selling that product or service to them.

The key difference when you work for yourself is that you're the head of sales *and* the head of marketing at the same time. Use your size to your advantage. By having oversight over both sales and marketing, you can streamline the entire process. There's no other department to liaise with so you can build an integrated process. There's more about sales in the next chapter but for now let's start by taking a deeper look at marketing.

Market research

Market research is the gathering of information about your potential customers or clients so that you can market to them effectively. It's a step you should take when developing any new business idea as it will also determine whether it's a viable one. It's also a step most freelancers skip over as they're so excited to just get started with their idea. Market research is the permission slip you need to make your idea a roaring success.

While this stage is vital, it's equally important not to get analysis paralysis. Don't delay moving forward with your marketing by conducting never-ending research. Instead focus your efforts on answering the following core questions:

- How big is the market for your product or service?
- What are the current trends in your industry?
- Who are your potential customers?
- Where are they?
- How do they like to be communicated with?
- What influences them to buy things?

You can find the answers to these questions in two ways: by speaking to your potential customers directly or by using public records and datasets to find the answers. It's best practice to use a combination of both in your researching efforts. In the 'Tools' section later in this chapter you'll find a list of resources you can use in your market research.

Marketing goals

Have you ever started a project only to realise halfway through that you don't know why you're doing it? The biggest pitfall with marketing your business is starting without knowing what you hope to achieve.

All freelancers will agree that marketing is important but few can pinpoint why they need to run consistent and effective marketing campaigns. For that reason, it's super important to nail down exactly what you want to get out of your marketing efforts. That way, you'll be able to develop strategies and then measure whether or not they worked for you. In other words, if you want to see your marketing efforts actually do something, first you need to set out your intentions.

There are four types of goals freelancers can aim for with their marketing efforts:

1. Generate sales leads – *find potential new customers you can sell to*
2. Retain existing customers – *keep your client happy so they stay loyal and continue to buy from you*
3. Increase brand awareness – *increase the recognition and reputation of your brand*
4. Develop thought leadership – *become recognised as an expert in your field*

Customer personas

If you're serious about nailing your marketing, you need to know who you're trying to target. By understanding your customers, you'll be better placed to create marketing strategies that appeal to them. You can do this by creating customer personas, which are fictionalised versions of your ideal customer or client. Some large marketing departments will mock this up with a cartoon sketch, or even photographs of real people, and give them names like Sally Student and Toby Teacher. When I was training to be a journalist, I was similarly taught to have a real person in mind while writing. By imagining who your customer is, you bring them to life and it becomes a lot easier to create something specifically for them.

Creating a customer persona is a lot of fun. I've sketched out little doodles of my customers. You can also use emojis for your personas' avatars. A tool like HubSpot's Make My Persona will create a persona for you (www.hubspot.com/make-my-persona) or you can make your own by using the questions below as prompts.

- How old are they?
- What industry do they work in?
- What social media sites do they use?
- What newspapers do they read? What TV shows do they watch? What podcasts do they listen to?
- How do they like to be communicated to? (Email, phone, social media?)
- What are their interests?
- What stores do they buy from?

This exercise is designed for F2C freelancers but you can also use it if you're F2B. The questions you'll ask will look slightly different: what do they do? Have you used their product? What is their business model? How do they make their money? What are their company values? Just like F2C freelancers need to understand their customers, F2B freelancers need to understand the company they're selling to.

Marketing strategies

A marketing strategy is the specific method you use to attract customers to your business or to grow awareness of your brand. It's the 'doing' bit of your marketing. There are countless marketing strategies you can use, from a simple social media campaign to a complex data-driven acquisition strategy.

When you work for yourself, it falls to you to devise your marketing strategies, often with few resources. With that in mind, I've outlined below the most relevant marketing strategies for freelancers and how to use them.

SEO

Search engine optimisation is the process of making sure you come up on the first page of Google when someone searches for you or your business. SEO is important for all freelancers, regardless of your industry, because it directly impacts how easy it is for customers to find you online.

SEO is a specialist skill which you can pay an expert or agency to handle for you but the majority of freelancers can take care of their own SEO by following a few basic steps. The first thing to do is to get your head around keywords and to use them effectively. Keywords are the common words and phrases people type into Google when they search for something. You want to find out what those keywords are and make sure you're using them on your website, in blog posts and on social media. You can use Google's keyword planner tool (ads.google.com/intl/en_uk/home/tools/keyword-planner/) to find your keywords. Compile a list and include them frequently in your online content.

You then want to make sure the backend of your website is SEOed to the nines. This means filling out the meta tags section and using clear headings, as well as peppering keywords throughout your pages. If this is something you struggle with, consider hiring a freelance website copywriter. They'll be able to go over all your website copy to ensure it's SEO friendly.

Lastly, keeping your content fresh will help you rank highly in search engine results. Google and other search engines favour content that's updated regularly, so if you have a blog, make sure you post new content frequently.

Social media

As a freelancer, social media is one of the most powerful tools at your disposal. Nearly 4 billion people currently use social media and that figure is only projected to increase. Whether you like it or not, social media is the best tool you have for promoting your business of one.

Your social media strategy will be largely informed by what outcome you want to achieve. The goal isn't necessarily to hit a certain number of followers on Instagram or Twitter but rather to raise awareness of your brand or to attract people who actually want to buy from you. This doesn't mean churning out content for the sake of it but instead using social media as a tool to connect with like-minded customers and clients.

Start by deciding which platform is right for you, as you really don't have to be everywhere. A TikTok account probably won't be relevant for an architect but will be more suitable for a makeup artist. Similarly, a hairdresser doesn't need a LinkedIn account but a consultant does. Refer back to your market research and customer personas to figure out which platforms your customers use and set up shop there.

Content marketing

Content marketing helps you build a relationship with your audience. It's a long-term strategy that uses engaging content to create brand awareness and loyalty. If you think about how traditional advertising gets something *out* of the audience, content marketing is supposed to *give them* something valuable. That's why it's important to stress this is a long-term strategy; you can't deploy a content marketing strategy and expect short-term results as you might do with paid advertising. The goal of content marketing is to build trust with your audience by giving them value.

A simple of way of doing this is on social media. If you post things that your followers find relevant and engaging, they will start to see you as a go-to source of information. Here are some examples:

- **Giveaways:** The author Laura Jane Williams runs Instagram contests in which the winner gets to name a character in her next novel.
- **User-generated content:** Share pictures of your work in action. Pria Bhamra, a freelance nail artist, fills her feed with pictures of her nail art. She uses Instagram Stories to repost photos her clients have taken themselves.
- **Memes:** Alice Tapper, the founder of personal finance service Go Fund Yourself, slays at creating hilarious memes about money, resulting in a 35,000-strong Instagram community of loyal followers.
- **Accountability exercises:** Every Monday, the journalist, coach and public speaker Harriet Minter posts a photo

on her Instagram of five things. In the caption she shares five things she plans to achieve that week and asks her followers to comment the same.

- **Q&As:** The author Emma Gannon uses Instagram's Q&A function to connect with her audience and build an engaged following.

There are plenty of other ways to use content marketing in your business of one. Here are some examples:

- **Newsletters:** Online entrepreneur Sara Tasker sends a monthly newsletter in which she shares insights about Instagram relevant to her followers.
- **Blog posts:** The graphic designer Louise O'Kane writes blog posts about navigating the world of design for business owners.
- **Videos:** The makeup artist Lisa Eldridge posts makeup tutorials on her YouTube channel. She uses her own products and teaches a technique rather than just demonstrating how to use them.

Lead magnets

A lead magnet is a freebie, usually in the form of a download, in exchange for a customer's contact details. While content marketing is a soft approach to enticing potential customers, lead magnets are an immediate exchange – the customer 'buys' your lead magnet with their email address, which you can then use to sell them your products or services.

Just like with content marketing, the freebie has to be your best work. People need to see value as they're giving you their precious email address. Targeted content with a specific niche does particularly well as a lead magnet because it really homes in on your audience. This makes it a great strategy for online businesses trying to grow their potential customer base.

Here are some examples of lead magnets. All of the ideas below require the customer to provide their email address in order to access or download the content.

- **Guides and ebooks:** I have a PDF guide to going freelance for people who've just lost their jobs.
- **Templates:** The relationship coach and *New York Times* bestselling author Matthew Hussey offers downloadable text templates for women in the early stages of dating.
- **Workbook:** As an incentive to sign up for her newsletter, the content marketing expert Jennifer Goforth Gregory offers a free downloadable worksheet on increasing your income in 60 days.
- **Webinar:** The online entrepreneur Danielle Leslie uses webinars and pre-filmed videos to promote her online training workshops.

Paid advertising

Paying to place ads for your services is one of the oldest marketing techniques in the book. Facebook and Google offer powerful digital advertising options, which allow you to hyper-target an audience on a small budget. Depending on your line of work, there's still value in the traditional advertising options, such as classified sections. Again, whether posting an ad in a local paper will work for you or not comes down to what your market research yielded – if your potential customers read the local paper to find a bookkeeper, then you should advertise your bookkeeping services there.

Before you part with any money, set your goals. As I mentioned above, any marketing effort needs to have a clear goal in mind. What do you want to achieve with your paid advertising campaign? If you want to increase sales, your approach will look different than if you want to raise awareness of your brand. Once you have your goals set, make a budget. How much can you afford to put into a paid advertising campaign and what does a good return on investment look like? Your aim is to recoup the cost of what you paid in advertising by acquiring new customers. Putting this all together, if you're running an event and your goal is to sell more tickets, you need to work out if the cost of paying for an advert will bring in enough ticket sales to make it worth the investment.

Partnerships

Borrow a proven marketing strategy from large companies and use co-branding partnerships to cross-pollinate your marketing with another freelancer. Co-branding partnerships are when two companies come together to produce a joint product or service. Think of Kanye collaborating with Adidas on his line of Yeezy trainers or Heston Blumenthal working with Waitrose on a line of speciality food. You don't have to be a large multinational, however, to benefit from a joint venture. Individual freelancers can easily work together to complement their skills and market themselves to each other's audiences.

Here are some ideas to get you started:

- **Co-hosted events:** I've run an online masterclass about launching a newsletter with fellow freelancer and email expert Sian Meades-Williams. We marketed the event to our audiences, which had enough cross-over to make the partnership a natural fit but were also different enough to bring in new customers, resulting in us selling out the event.
- **Guest appearance:** Freelance hairdresser Jess B Cruz regularly hosts the nail artist Pria Bhamra in her studio space. The pair advertise the guest appearance on their respective Instagram accounts. Getting your nails done goes hand-in-hand with a hair appointment so slots quickly fill up.
- **Social media collaborating:** The mummy blogger and lifestyle influencer Louise Pentland filmed her mentee and professional organiser Super Scrimping Soph organising her wardrobe for her. Louise got relevant content for her social media channels and Sophie raised awareness of her business.

Letters of introduction

A letter of introduction is an email you send a prospective client introducing yourself and your services to them.

Letters of introduction are an important marketing strategy for freelancers in the creative services industry, such as writers, illustrators, consultants and videographers.

Once you've researched companies to approach for this kind of work, keep your email short and to the point. You need no more than three paragraphs: an opening one that makes it clear you're getting in touch to enquire about freelance work opportunities; another paragraph outlining your relevant experience that makes you attractive to them; and then a concluding paragraph letting them know you have ideas and you're ready to send them over.

Tailor your pitch accordingly. You might want to highlight similar work you've done in the past. If you have any snappy metrics to show your results – for example, a link to a testimonial or some figures that demonstrate how you helped a similar client – include them. Here's an example of a letter of introduction:

Dear Potential New Client,

My name's Anna and I'm getting in touch to ask if your company works with freelance writers? I've seen on your website that you have a blog and I would love to contribute to it if you're open to pitches.

I'm a freelancer who writes about business, culture and technology. I specialise in the future of work, the freelance economy and flexible working. My writing has appeared in the New York Times, Guardian, Wired *and* Monocle. *(I've included links to a few clips at the bottom of this email.)*

*I have some ideas that I think would be a great fit
for your blog; if you're interested in hearing them, I'll
happily send them over.*

Thank you,

Anna

Publicity

When you earn media, also known as publicity or public
relations (PR), someone else talks up your business on your
behalf. This usually happens in the form of writeups in the
press, social media influencers recommending your services
(without you paying them to do so) and happy customers
recommending you to friends. You can't pay for this coverage and generally it happens organically but you can increase
your chances of gaining earned media.

- **Follow journalists:** Create a list of relevant journalists who
  cover your industry and follow them on social media.
- **Send a press release:** A press release can be a short
  email to relevant editors letting them know about your
  new venture.
- **Hire a freelance PR agent:** If you're serious about
  getting press coverage, you don't need a big
  international firm to do your PR. You can consider
  hiring a freelancer.

Websites, online portfolios and directory listings

Having a digital presence across the internet is important.
Remember, however, that simply creating a website is not a
marketing strategy in itself. You then need to do the work

to actually get people to find it, look at it and do something about it. That's where a combination of the strategies listed above comes in.

While I do think that all freelancers need a website to help clients find them, I don't believe it should be your first priority by a long stretch. If you want a website that's actually going to help you market your business, you need to invest time and money into it. Even if you don't design your website yourself, you'll still need to find someone else to do it for you and you'll need to brief them thoroughly to make sure they do it well. Platforms like Squarespace, WordPress, Wix and Webflow offer pre-built website templates that you can customise but to get it looking good will take a lot of your time. If you set up your website yourself, it will cost you about £100 a year in hosting and domain fees (plus your own time). If you hire a web designer to create it for you, you're looking at anywhere between £500 and upwards of £2,000 depending on how complex you need it to be.

What your website needs:

- A clear homepage explaining who you are and what you do. This can be as simple as a sentence that summarises your work and a picture.
- An 'about' page containing more details and your bio. This should explain what services you offer.
- A contact page so your customers know how to get in touch and follow you on social media – this is obviously very important!
- Samples of your work.

In addition to a website, if you run a consumer-facing freelance business, list it in public business directories.

The largest one is Google My Business, a free tool that allows you to promote your business on Google, so it shows up in search results and on maps. It's also worth adding your details to local or specialist directories. Listing your details in directories is especially important for freelancers whose clients are likely to find them by Googling them, for example, hairdressers, nail artists, florists and architects.

As for client service-based work, freelance talent networks are online platforms you can submit your portfolio to and, if accepted, you'll be matched with clients. The advantage of these sites over marketplaces is that the calibre of clients is higher, as are the rates of pay. An account manager typically manages the freelancer's work, which means clear workflows and deadlines. Another major advantage of these sites is that often they have payment systems built directly into the platform so you will get paid instantly upon submitting your work (usually via a service such as PayPal). You can also use these sites solely to create a portfolio that you can send to potential clients.

The freelancer's five-point marketing plan

The most effective way to take your marketing to the next level is by putting together a marketing plan. I'm a fan of keeping my plans short and to the point. I use a five-point plan for all my marketing needs in my business of one. It covers everything I need and fits onto one piece of paper. I create a marketing plan whenever I launch a new income stream and continue to review it as my business grows. I'll walk you through how to create your own:

1. Goal – *which of the four marketing goals are you working towards?*
2. Target – *what specifically do you want to achieve and by when?*
3. Strategy – *what approach will you take to reach your target?*
4. Steps – *what are the detailed steps you're going to take to execute your strategy?*
5. Results – *how are you going to measure your success?*

Examples

A freelance writer is launching a newsletter with recipes for first-time mums and wants to attract new readers. Her marketing strategy is to use social media to grow her readership.

Goal: Raise brand awareness

Target: Get 100 new email sign-ups to my newsletter by 31 October

Strategy: Social media (Twitter campaign)

Steps:

1. Update my Twitter bio to clearly explain what my newsletter is and include a link for readers to sign up.
2. Post daily content relevant to first-time mums to build a following around my subject area and become known as a go-to resource for this audience.
3. Post three tweets a week about my newsletter, explaining what readers will get if they sign up, and include a clear call to action with a sign-up link.
4. Find other people in the first-time mum community to follow. Engage with them on Twitter, contributing to conversations and sharing my insights.

Results: At the end of the month, measure how many new sign-ups I attracted. Use tracking links in my tweets to see which ones drove more sign-ups. Analyse what worked and what didn't.

An independent greetings card maker wants to grow her business over the summer months when demand for cards is lower than in the winter. She has a small budget to use paid advertising to encourage her existing customers to buy more cards from her.

Goal: Retain existing customers

Target: Get 20 new sales from existing customers by 1 June

Strategy: Paid advertising (Instagram campaign)

Steps:

1. Create an Instagram advert using a striking image of one of my most popular cards and include a call to action to buy now.
2. Target previous customers so that I reach the right people with my ads.
3. Run the campaign for one month, monitoring its progress as it goes along and making any necessary tweaks.

Results: Each week, take a look at your analytics dashboard in Instagram to see how many people saw the ad. Also track how many people went on to buy a card as a result of seeing the ad. Analyse the insights that Instagram provides to see what worked and what didn't.

A business consultant wants to land three new clients by the end of the month. Her strategy is to send letters of interest to cold and warm leads to promote her services.

Goal: Generate sales leads
Target: Get three new clients for my corporate wellbeing consulting business by the end of the month
Strategy: Letters of introduction
Steps:

1. Write a template email.
2. Make a list of previous clients and send them a tailored version of my letter of introduction.
3. Follow up after one week. If they reply saying they don't have any work for me, ask for an introduction to someone else in their company or network who might.
4. Make a list of ten companies in my niche I'd like to work with.
5. Find the head of employee wellbeing at those companies and send them a tailored version of the email.
6. Follow up on the emails after a week.

Results: At the end of the month, assess how many new clients I landed after sending my letters of introduction. Analyse how many were from my existing contacts and network compared to cold leads.

Tools

The more organised you are, the more you'll get out of your marketing plan. Here are the types of tools you'll need to keep on top of your marketing.

Project management: You'll want a system for planning out your marketing efforts and keeping track of all the elements in your marketing plan. Project management tools like Trello, Asana, Notion and Monday.com are great for creating content calendars, tracking projects and even collaborating with team-mates so you can stay on top of your marketing plan.

Research and analytics: Before you launch into a marketing campaign, you need to research thoroughly. Find data and statistics on sites including the Office of National Statistics, Pew Research Center and Statista. Use Google Trends, and the free industry reports from Gartner and McKinsey to track trends. And after you've executed your plan you need to analyse what happened. You can create tracking links using Bit.ly and see how many people visited your website using Google Analytics.

Schedulers: Posting on social media doesn't have to mean sitting on Twitter all day. Automate your marketing as much as possible by scheduling your posts in advance. Tools like Later, Hootsuite and Buffer offer both free and paid versions for managing your social media accounts, including scheduling, analytics and running ads.

Email newsletters: When you have a customer's email address, you can speak to them directly. This is valuable for all sorts of freelancers, whether you're selling directly to your customers or building an audience. Tools like MailChimp, ConvertKit and MailerLite allow you to build email lists which you can segment and target for specific email campaigns. You can also automate your marketing efforts with these platforms' advanced features. If you're writing an editorial newsletter, platforms like Substack, TinyLetter and Revue will help you grow your readership.

Design software: You don't need a degree in design to create a cohesive online visual identity. Many people hire a freelance designer but if you want to create your own, there are plenty of free tools that will help you easily create all your marketing assets. Use Unsplash for free images, Canva for creating social media posts and Squarespace, Wordpress or Wix for pre-designed website templates.

Chapter Summary: DIY Marketing

If you want to stop the feast-and-famine of freelancing, invest in consistent marketing efforts and clients will find you.

Marketing vs sales: Remember, *marketing comes before sales*. Marketing is the process of finding potential customers for your product or service and then sales is the act of selling that product or service to them.

Marketing strategies: From earned media and letters of interest to social media and content marketing, pick a marketing strategy that works for your business.

The freelancer's five-point marketing plan: Set a goal; determine what you want to achieve and by when; define your approach; outline the steps you're going to take to execute your strategy; measure your success.

FREELANCER STORY

Pria Bhamra (@bhambnails) – celebrity nail artist

I started out working in nail salons, which was a great place to learn and develop but the pay and zero-hours contracts meant it was unsustainable for the long term.

I took an office job to earn a regular pay cheque while I built up my client base in the evenings and on weekends. Eventually, I left that office job but was too scared to go all-in on freelancing, even though I did have a few consistent clients at that point. So, instead, I took a part-time job at another salon and continued to work with my private clients on the side.

But the same thing happened – poor pay and long hours. This time, however, I realised that what I was getting in a salon in a day I'd make in a couple of hours with my clients. That's when I asked myself, why am I still doing this? And at that point, I'd built up enough clients to feel confident in deciding it was time to just go for it. That was two years ago and things really took off after that.

Instagram plays a huge role in my business. Every day, I post pictures of all the nails I've done for my clients. When I started posting regularly like that, my account grew and led me to new clients. Now that I'm more established, I get work through word of mouth but when I first started, Instagram was the main source of new clients. Some of my clients are influencers, which also helped me build my own business because they'll post pictures of their nails to their large followings. I'm also fortunate to work with some celebrity clients, which is great because they tend to get their nails done every week or two. Not only is the work consistent but it's also fun because celebrities never want plain nails. They always want bold designs. I love working on those creative projects.

CHAPTER SEVEN

Selling Your Skills

I have good news and bad news when it comes to selling. Let's start with the bad: you have to do it. There's no way to run a business and not to sell anything. The good news, however, is that anyone can do it. Selling is a skill that can be taught; you just have to believe you can learn it.

Over 30 years ago, the American psychologist Carol Dweck set out to understand students' attitudes to failure. Her research led her to develop an entirely new way of understanding how we learn skills. It all comes down to our beliefs and whether we have a fixed or growth mindset. A fixed mindset is the belief that we are born with certain skills and attributes that can't be changed, whereas if we have a growth mindset, we believe that we can learn anything we put our minds to. Cultivating a growth mindset has transformed my abilities as a freelancer and owner of a business of one. It's especially come into its own when I was trying to master selling, something I thought I was innately bad at. Simply believing that I could find a way to get good at sales laid the groundwork for me to then learn the art of sales. Now, I'm not going to pretend that there's a magic pill you can take and suddenly wake up as an expert salesperson. I know from my own experiences that building the sales muscle takes time and effort, but I also know that it can be done.

It took nearly having to close an arm of my freelancing business for me to realise how desperately I needed to address my sales skills. The model for my subscription-based newsletter, as I explained earlier, only works if a percentage of the readers pay to become premium members. Even launching it in the first place was a big deal for me – the concept of paid-for newsletters was in its infancy back then (and still is now) and the prospect of asking people to pay me to send them an email was daunting enough to nearly stop me from doing it at all. But I bit the bullet and enough people signed up straight away to show me it was a viable business idea.

Once the initial buzz wore off, however, I focused solely on making sure the content was high quality and serving readers well. And then the pandemic hit and subscriptions started to drop as people reined in their spending. I watched this happen, feeling powerless. There was nothing I could do to stem the haemorrhaging of subscribers, I thought. Until I realised that there was in fact something I could do – I could try to sell new subscriptions.

It was true that some people didn't want to keep up their subscriptions but there were other people out there who might want to subscribe for the first time and I needed to find them. I took an honest look at what I was doing and realised I'd completely neglected my sales strategy for some time. I was using the pandemic as an excuse when, in reality, I hadn't done anything to improve my sales for months leading up to that point.

What was stopping me? Honestly, it came down to a fear of looking greedy. I always knew that the warmest leads I have to sell subscriptions to are the people on my free email list. They like my writing enough to sign up to receive a weekly email from me; it's not that much of a jump to ask them to pay to support that work and to receive even more content in return. And yet, I didn't want to upset them by asking them every now and then if they would.

I'm a planner, so I solved this problem by planning my way out of it. I started by setting myself a goal – I wanted to increase my premium subscribers by 20% within a month. I came up with a plan for how I was going to do this and I wrote it down in a Google doc, laying out the steps I needed to take. Then it was just a matter of following that plan. At the end of the month, my subscribers were up by 15%. I took at a look at what had worked and what hadn't, and I made another plan for the next month. I repeated the whole thing again.

Accepting that selling had to happen in my business made the world of difference to my sales skills. You have to accept that selling is part of your business. It's another business function, just like doing your taxes and paying bills. You might not like them, but they have to get done. Rather than fighting against this, instead find ways to detach from it emotionally. I'm not saying you have to like selling but you really don't have to like something to accept it. You just need to find ways to get comfortable with it.

In my experience, the narrative you tell yourself about your sales abilities becomes a self-fulfilling prophecy. When I'd convinced myself I was bad at selling, I didn't sell much. But once I started telling myself that selling is a skill that I'm capable of learning (and then did the work to develop it), my sales went up. In this chapter, I'll walk you through the basics of selling and how to overcome everything that's held you back in the past.

What you'll learn in this chapter:

- Why people buy things
- The shy person's selling cheat sheet
- Sales strategies that won't make you feel icky
- A rinse-and-repeat sales process

People Buy Things for One Simple Reason

In the early 2000s, when McDonald's asked the late business school professor Clayton Christensen to help the fast-food chain sell more milkshakes, he had one goal in mind: to work out what job people were hiring their milkshakes to do. If that sounds strange, it's because it is a pioneering approach to consumer behaviour. Christensen had just developed a theory he called 'job to be done', which posited that when someone buys something, they're essentially 'hiring' that product or service to help them do a job. There are social, emotional and functional dimensions to jobs.

These 'jobs' can include anything from passing time while standing in a queue to finding a more fulfilling career. The theory was built on the Harvard Business School marketing professor Theodore Levitt's assertion that people don't want to buy a quarter-inch drill, they want a quarter-inch hole. They hire the drill to do a job for them. And yes, milkshakes do a job, too.

So, the question for Christensen became: what was the job? His research found that one of the main jobs people were hiring McDonald's milkshakes to do was to accompany them on long, lonely drives. This knowledge was immensely powerful because it meant that McDonald's were able to think completely differently about how to sell their shakes. One idea Christensen came up with was simply moving the milkshake dispenser in front of the counter for buyers in a hurry to access it faster.

The key to selling a product is to understand not only who the customer is but also what they're trying to accomplish. Understanding this and incorporating it into your business strategy not only increases your sales but also makes innovation possible. The impact of Christensen's job-to-be-done theory is as applicable to businesses of one as it is to conglomerates. Let's look at some examples of how this might apply to freelancers:

What job is someone hiring a makeup artist to do? Doing their makeup, sure, but there's more to it than that. Take for example a bride hiring a makeup artist for her wedding day; the job she's really hiring them to do is making her feel beautiful on her special day.

Why does someone hire an accountant? You might think it's to do their taxes but it's more likely to give them peace of mind that their taxes were filed correctly. So when you sell to them, focus on your credentials. Let them know they can be confident trusting their books to you.

What job is an editor hiring a freelance writer to do? On the surface the answer seems so obvious: to write an article. But dig deeper and you'll find the editor has their own job they need doing – they might have a mission they're trying to achieve, they might want to progress their own career or they might just want to look good in front of their boss.

Figuring out the *real* job that needs doing will reveal crucial information that you can use to sell to your customers. For example, the person who wants to hire the makeup artist to make them feel beautiful won't care where they trained or whether they're cheaper than the competitors. They just want to know you'll make them feel special. However, the person who wants to hire an accountant for peace of mind with their taxes probably *is* interested in their credentials as they'll inspire confidence. Understanding customers' emotional, social and functional jobs enables you to position your products and services to reflect what they are trying to do.

The Shy Person's Selling Cheat Sheet

You don't have to be a gregarious extrovert to be good at selling. I know this to be true because I'm a shy introvert and I can sell. However, if my meandering experiences aren't evidence enough, the Wharton Business School professor Adam Grant found that of all the personality types, it's actually ambiverts – those who are equal parts introvert and extrovert – who make the best salespeople.

Use your personality traits to your advantage. If you're shy, don't try to become someone you're not. Instead adapt your sales techniques to suit your personality. Ask a lot of questions and get the other person to do most of the talking. Repeat back to them what they're saying so they feel listened to and will engage further with you.

Here are my confidence-boosting cheats for mastering sales:

Rebrand selling

If you don't like the thought of selling, stop thinking of it as selling. It really is that simple! Instead, think of it as educating or sharing information. You aren't forcing anyone to buy something they don't want or need, you're just giving people the opportunity to choose something that might be right for them. If you don't like aggressive sales techniques, you don't have to use them. Selling doesn't have to mean recreating the scenes from *The Wolf of Wall Street*.

Believe in what you're selling

You don't necessarily have to believe in yourself but you do have to believe in what you're selling. The cheesy 1990s advice for salespeople was to look in the mirror and shout, 'I'm good at selling!' Even with the good intention of helping people grow their confidence, advice that relies on me telling myself I'm good at something never seems to work. Instead, I tell myself the thing I'm selling is good. I don't focus on believing in myself. I focus on believing in what I'm offering. This helps me get out of my own way and creates a bit of distance between me and the act of selling.

Watch other people sell to you and tune into the experience

When was the last time you were sold to? Start observing the experience and unpack what makes it a positive or negative one. It's unfair to come up with a blanket statement that you hate selling because you don't like being sold to as it's more than likely you've had countless positive experiences buying something.

Anyone can sell

Selling is a learnable skill but if you don't believe that to be true, you'll never be able to master it. I know that some of you reading this won't want to accept that anyone can get good at selling. As you'll see in this chapter, by understanding why people buy things, reframing how you view sales and creating a repeatable and reliable sales process, even you can get comfortable selling.

Non-gross Sales Strategies

The problem with a lot of sales tactics is that they're gross. To put it bluntly. If you've ever been on the receiving end of an aggressive sales approach, you'll know what I mean – you're dragged along by the salesperson's hunger for the close, not listened to at all. I had this experience recently with a mortgage broker who was trying to sell me her brokerage services. Even after I told her I'd decided to go with a different broker, that didn't seem to stop her. She called me a week later to try and sell me mortgage life insurance. As a first-time homeowner, I had no clue what this insurance meant, not to mention I hadn't even completed the house sale yet, but what I did know was that she was pushing me to buy something I wasn't ready for.

In 2013, the author Daniel H. Pink gave the art of selling a much needed makeover. In his bestseller *To Sell Is Human: The surprising truth about moving others*, he outlined the new ABC of selling as: attunement, buoyancy and clarity. Attunement is the ability to see things from someone else's perspective, understanding what makes them tick. Buoyancy is the resilience to stay afloat in an 'ocean of rejection'. Clarity is being able to untangle complexities, not only to solve existing problems but also to dig deeper and find hidden ones.

At the heart of Pink's modern-day sales manifesto is an acute focus on listening to what your potential customer is trying to tell you. Ditch the pushy tactics, stop treating sales like a blood sport and instead be a human about it. If you want to be comfortable selling, learn how to sell in a way that you'd like to be sold to and deploy a non-gross sales strategy instead.

The easiest way to do this is by asking good questions of your potential customers and then actively listening to the answer. As a trained journalist, I've mastered the art of asking questions over the years. I use these techniques now in my sales process to better understand what my customers and clients want.

Talk less, listen more. As tempting as it is to jump in and finish the other person's sentence for them, don't. Just let them talk. Not only will they feel listened to but they may very well share a golden nugget of information with you.

Ask open-ended questions. Ask questions that can't be answered with one word. For example, 'Can you tell me about your business?'; 'What are your top priorities in your business right now?'; 'What challenges do you face in achieving your priorities?'; 'Why is this a priority for you now?';

'How do you evaluate new products or services before buying them?'

Have two to three 'big' questions in mind. Go into your conversation with your big questions prepared in advance. These might be things like, 'What would it take for you to hire me to carry out this project?' or 'Why do you buy products from my competitor?'. You don't have to ask these questions in exactly the way they're worded here but your mission is to find the answers to them in your conversation.

When they say something that's clearly important to them, repeat it back to them. This simple act of mimicry will not only make the other person warm to you, it will also prompt them to keep talking.

Power phrases. One of my favourite sentences to say in any interview is 'Tell me more about that.' This simple phrase signals to the other person that you know what they've said is important and you want to hear more about it. 'Can you give me an example?' is another useful phrase as it encourages the other person to articulate their problem by sharing a real-life example of it.

Why You Need a Simple Sales Process and How to Build One

The concept of a pre-written sales process isn't new. If you've ever worked in telesales, you'll be familiar with the scripts you're given to sell a product or service over the phone.

You want to create a simple sales process for your business to give you some much needed emotional distance. When there's something in my business that causes me stress,

I create a repeatable process for it. I'm going to walk you through my tried-and-tested sales process here. Don't worry, this isn't a lesson in sales funnels or flywheels. This is just a simple process breaking down the three key steps you need to take when delivering a sale.

Identify

The first step in your sales process is the most important one. You need to identify potential customers and clients – something that's called 'prospecting' in sales lingo. Your goal here is to find people who have a need for your product or service and who also have the decision-making ability to buy it from you. You cannot move on to the next step in your sales process until this criterion is met in full. It's no good finding someone who wants to hire you as a freelance graphic designer but doesn't have the authority to do so.

This is where your marketing efforts come into play. They'll be your first port of call for identifying the right person to sell to. If you've used lead magnets or content marketing, you might have built up an email list of potential customers. If you've been using social media to build an audience, there might be names of people in your list of followers who want to buy your services. You can also use your network, Google and email outreach to identify your sales prospects.

Prepare

Once you've figured out who you're going to sell to, you then need to prep for your sale. This stage is the 'warming' phase; your goal here is to prepare your client to be sold to.

The reason you need to do this is simply to avoid wasting your own time. In the early days of my freelancing journey, I would find myself in meetings which I thought were going to lead to me being hired for a freelance project but turned out to be brain-picking sessions. What I thought was a potential client would get in touch with me and I'd agree to their request to meet for a coffee. I'd go along thinking I'd get some work out of the meeting but all I got was the coffee. I soon realised the problem was that I hadn't prepared my potential client for being sold to. The best way to do this is by being clear. Now I say upfront, 'I'd like to meet with you to talk about how we can work together.'

If this stage happens over the phone or in person, you'll want to ask those open-ended questions listed above. And don't forget to listen carefully to the answers, repeating back the key pieces of information the potential client shares with you. It's also worth writing these answers down for your own research purposes. Most clients tend to have the same sorts of problems so it can be good to start identifying patterns.

Sell

The final step is the sale itself. In some cases, this might be a physical pitch meeting or a proposal delivered over the phone. In others, it's an email that's more about finalising the details after laying the foundations in the first two steps. In any case, it's at this stage you want to put your 'Job to Be Done' strategy into practice. This is where you want to make clear to your customer or client how you're going to solve their problems for them.

Sales process examples

In practice, these steps can come together in a number of different ways. You might do all three steps virtually, selling over email and through websites and never speaking to a customer or client directly. Or you might meet face to face a number of times before agreeing to a sale. Here are three different examples of how the sales process can play out:

A freelance makeup artist's sales process for selling a wedding makeup package to a customer

Identify: Market your services where you know clients are most likely to look for you. In the case of makeup artistry, Instagram can be a great shop window for you. Include a clear call to action in your bio, directing potential customers to an enquiry form or another means to contact you.

Prepare: When customers get in touch, offer a trial session, which is chargeable but redeemable against products in order to give them a sense of what will happen on the big day. Ask them lots of questions about what they hope their day will look like and what would make them most comfortable. Show them you're listening carefully by repeating back anything important they share with you.

Sell: Call the client after a week to follow up. At this point you want to emphasise you can do the job they want done and that you listened to what they needed. If they mentioned to you in the trial session that they are worried about getting flustered on the day, let them know how you'll make them feel pampered and taken care of on their special day. Sign the contract, book the date and take a deposit!

A freelance accountant's sales process for selling an accounting package to a small business owner

Identify: Find business owners who need your help. Start by reaching out to business owners in your network to ask if they're happy with their bookkeeping and accounting set-up. You can also search for businesses in your niche on LinkedIn in order to expand your outreach.

Prepare: If the business owner replies to your email with interest, schedule an initial phone call with them. The purpose of this call is to find out how they're doing their accounting at the moment, what challenges they're facing and how you could best help them.

Sell: Once you're clear on what the potential client wants, send them a follow-up email with details of how you would handle their accounting for them. If they raised any specific requirements on the call, make sure to show how you'll fulfil them. Also let them know their books are in safe hands with you, highlighting your credentials and any long-standing clients you work with to inspire confidence.

A freelance writer's sales process for selling a feature to a magazine

Identify: Find the right editor. Your first step is to identify editors with commissioning power at publications that run similar stories to the one you'd like to write. If you've built a social media following, look through your contacts to find editors already following you to see if they fit the bill. A simple search on Twitter will also help you identify your ideal client.

Prepare: Selling freelance articles to editors is a well trodden sales path and steps two and three pretty much merge into one as they typically both happen over email. It's at this stage that you send your pitch. You want to be clear on why you're the right person to write this story, what access you have to interview subjects and your proven track record of delivering this kind of work.

Sell: This step is about agreeing the finer points of the commission, including negotiating the price and agreeing to the terms of the project. The editor might have some questions for you before they agree to the commission, at which point you want to lean on your selling strategies to get your pitch over the line. Answer these questions from the point of view of the job the editor needs to get done. Let's assume their job to get done is looking good in front of their boss. In that case, let them know you can deliver a brilliant story on time for them.

Solo sales meetings

Something you'll notice I've emphasised throughout this book is the importance of considering all the work you do as part of your freelance business as valuable. It is with that philosophy in mind that I say: put aside regular time for sales.

Too often freelancers are apprehensive about carrying out 'non-billable' work. If you're not getting paid for something directly, why should you prioritise it? Because while everything you do in your business needs to add value, that value won't always be immediately measurable in financial terms. Sure, no one is paying you for the hour it might take you to work on your LinkedIn profile but if that time leads to a three-month contract then that hour of 'unpaid work' has significant value to your business. The skill lies in learning how to determine what tasks are valuable. For example, a freelance hairdresser might not get the same value out of updating their LinkedIn profile as a freelance accountant might. For an accountant, spending a work morning on Instagram is probably not the best use of their time; for a hairdresser, it might be central to their marketing strategy.

Put time aside to regularly take care of your sales. Find a rhythm that works for you – personally, I do my sales work on a monthly basis but you might find a different schedule suits you better. I think of this time as my monthly sales meeting. Just as I would if I worked in a big sales team, I go over which new clients I've brought in over the last month and which prospective clients I can go after the following month.

Whether you do this exercise weekly, monthly or quarterly, make sure to use the time to figure out what worked when you approached your last client and how you can replicate that with your next one. You can be as organised and formal as you like. Don't get bogged down in things like what tools to use to track this information – a simple Word document, basic spreadsheet or even a notebook will suffice. The point here is to train yourself to do this regularly and to get comfortable with it.

How to Put Your Marketing and Sales Together

As I said in the previous chapter, marketing comes before sales. Marketing is the process of finding the potential customers for your product or service and then sales is the act of selling that product or service to them.

There are many areas of business where being small is a disadvantage but happily sales and marketing are not two of them. In fact, being a business of one means you can avoid a common problem larger companies have with the marketing and sales departments clashing with one another. The line between marketing and sales doesn't matter so much when it's just you and there's a lot of crossover between the two functions. If your marketing efforts are paying off you'll see this straight away, as they'll be delivering you the leads you need to initiate your sales process.

That's not to say there aren't ways to make sure your marketing and sales strategies are working as best as they can together. For instance, you might make strides with your marketing efforts only to not follow through with your sales. This was exactly what was happening with my newsletter – I was marketing the free version on social media and gaining earned media when readers forwarded the email to their friends but failing to see that the names on that free list were warm leads. The people most likely to start paying to receive my newsletter were the ones already signed up to the free version of it. I wasn't building my sales strategy on the foundations my marketing efforts had laid for me.

The same is true the other way around – what happens in your sales should be feeding back into your marketing plans. What worked and what didn't work in a sale is valuable information that you can loop back into your marketing efforts. For example, when I learned that many of the people who bought tickets to my events had done so after attending a previous event of mine, I focused my marketing efforts on previous attendees rather than trying to find new people to market to. It's only by measuring things that you'll learn from your mistakes.

Chapter Summary: Selling Your Skills

By accepting that selling is a crucial part of your business, you'll be able to start detaching from it emotionally and learn how to do it in a way that doesn't leave you feeling icky.

People buy things to get a job done: Working to understand your clients' and customers' emotional, social and functional needs means you'll be able to position your products and services to fulfil what they're trying to achieve.

Anyone can sell. They just have to believe it's possible to learn: It's not true that you have to be an extrovert to sell. Use your personality traits to your advantage and focus on sales techniques that you would respond well to yourself.

Ask better questions: If you want to sell in a way that doesn't make you uncomfortable, start by listening to what your potential customer is trying to tell you. Ask open-ended questions, use power phrases and don't be afraid of silence.

Simplify your sales process: By creating a simple sales process, you'll give yourself some much needed emotional distance. Remember to identify customers who have a need for your product/service and the decision-making ability to buy it from you; prepare them to be sold to; and only after those steps do you start selling.

FREELANCER STORY

Tiffany Philippou (@tiffphilippou) – writer, coach, podcaster and consultant

I'm a career-change freelancer who has a few different jobs. I went freelance after I got fired from my job as the head of brand and marketing at a startup, but the transition to self-employment wasn't immediate. I didn't think freelancing was an option for me at first and I was using my time off to explore pursuing a completely new career, either in politics or teaching, when a former colleague got in touch with a freelance job opportunity. My very first client project was a branding workshop, which was something I'd never done before. It went really well and things started to flow from there, with most of my new business coming from my existing network.

Given my background in marketing, I decided to start self-publishing my own content to market my consulting services. I wrote a blog post about how I turned my rebellious spirit into a job, which was a mission statement of sorts, but also a piece of writing about my life. The post got a lot of traction online and spurred me to keep blogging. I found I loved writing so much that I decided to find a way to incorporate it into my work. I started writing a weekly newsletter, pitched articles to magazines and even landed a book deal. More recently, I trained as a business coach. It's a natural extension of the work that I do, a good way to gain insights for my writing and another way to impact and help people.

My startup background, which taught me the principle of 'done is better than perfect', gave me the confidence to design my career in this way. I do believe that as a freelancer, you're an entrepreneur. That's why sales is such an important skill to master when running your own business. You're always selling your work. It's down to you to believe in that work – because who else will believe in it for you?

It might look like I do four jobs from the outside but the core that unites everything is a fascination with counter-narratives and wanting to challenge perceptions. All my work, whether it's my writing, coaching or consulting, is driven by that purpose. A lot of people do just one of the jobs I do full-time, whereas I'm trying to navigate doing them at the same time but still doing them well. It's definitely challenging, but at the same time, it bends and stretches me. Am I still using my rebellious spirit in my job? Well, I don't have a boss to rebel against anymore but I am doing things my own way now.

Part Two:

Freelance Life

CHAPTER EIGHT

Looking After Yourself

The irony is not lost on me that as I'm writing this chapter on taking care of yourself, the world is in the middle of a global pandemic. The Covid-19 crisis gave me a badly wrapped gift: a lesson in what it really means to look after your physical and mental health when you work for yourself. When lockdown first came into effect, I assumed not a lot would change in my life. I already worked from home, as did my partner, so I was used to blending my working and personal lives. It was only when my days started to unravel that I realised how I hadn't put any protocols in place for coping in a crisis. Not only that but it turned out that my self-care foundation was quite shaky, too.

I didn't understand where this unravelling had come from as I'd led myself to believe I was a pillar of wellbeing. I used to get up early and start each day with an involved morning routine that included a gratitude practice, bullet journaling and calendar-blocking my diary to maximise every moment. I told myself I was doing these things because they were good for me and counted as 'self-care'. But in reality, I mainly did them because I was trying to optimise myself for work. As an organised person, the concept of a flexible schedule was an oxymoron as far as I was concerned. The pandemic made me realise I was throttling myself with my rigidity and that I needed a schedule that left me enough room to breathe.

I've since learned to ditch rigid routines in favour of rituals and my days look very different now. A routine is practical and focused on getting things done, while a ritual is about finding meaning in the action itself. While both are a series of steps or actions, they foster different mindsets. To start with, I wake up without an alarm, relying on my body to tell me when it's time to get up, basking in one of the true luxuries of working for yourself. Then I take the dogs out for a walk, making sure to leave my phone behind so I'm actually present and focused.

When I get back, I make my tea and sit down to write down what I need from my day. This is categorically not a to-do list (more on that later) but a handwritten list in a notebook and one of my favourite rituals. I use this exercise to figure out what my needs are and how I'm going to meet them. For example, I might write, 'Today I need to honour my body by working out before starting my working day,' or I might write, 'Today I need to feel a sense of achievement by making progress on a challenging work task.' Some days my lists are five points long, other days there's only one point.

I'll still write down a few things I'm grateful for because expressing daily gratitude has been transformative for me but I now do it to actually feel grateful, rather than just to be able to get more work done. Then, depending on what I wrote on my needs list, I'll go about my day in a number of different possible ways. Some days, I'll jump straight into work. Others, I'll meditate, work out or read first.

As for my to-do list, I still have one because I couldn't – nor do I want to – abandon organisation completely. I've just rebranded it as my 'can-do' list. I used to write epic to-do lists, which only set me up for failure because there weren't enough hours in the day to complete all my tasks. Now, I write can-do at the top of my list and it prompts me to think about what's actually achievable with my time.

I now try to go about my days with intention. Days no longer happen to me; I don't look at my watch in the evenings and wonder where the hours went. Seemingly radical habits like waking up without an alarm have actually helped me get more done in a day than before, plus I feel so much better for it. This chapter will help you also take charge of your well-being, so your time feels like yours again.

In this chapter, you'll learn:

- How to spot the signs of burnout
- Resilience building strategies
- Tips for combating isolation

Freelancer Burnout

Before I went freelance, I worked as a news editor at an online media company in New York. I loved my job, but it was tough. For starters, I struggled with the American office's presenteeism culture. I requested to work from home one day a week but that was declined because the expectation was for us to be physically at our desks during working hours. On top of that, my job was highly reactionary; there was no way to set boundaries around my inbox because I needed to be alert to any breaking news situations. Not to mention the stories I covered were distressing – terrorist attacks, fires and drug-related deaths.

About six months in, I started feeling super tired all the time. After a while, a resentment towards my job crept over me. I felt like the energy I was putting into it wasn't being valued; I felt underappreciated and cynical towards my employer. Eventually, I began to feel like I wasn't even any good at my job.

I didn't realise it at the time but I was utterly burned out.

But working for yourself is by no means a fix for burnout. If anything, the precarity of self-employment and the dissolving boundaries between work and home are a breeding ground for it. On top of that, freelancers are caught in a painful double-bind – in order to get work, we need to put ourselves out there but in doing so, we face rejections that knock our confidence.

Left untreated, burnout can lead to depression and other mental health conditions. So, it's vital to get clear on what burnout actually is in order to spot the symptoms in yourself. The World Health Organisation classifies burnout as an occupational phenomenon, defining it as a syndrome 'resulting from chronic workplace stress that has not been successfully managed'.

The three symptoms of burnout are:

1. Feelings of energy depletion or exhaustion
2. Increased mental distance from one's job or feelings of negativity or cynicism related to one's job
3. Reduced personal efficacy

What distinguishes burnout from conditions like depression and anxiety is its relationship to work. While people who suffer from mental health conditions may find their ability to work affected, burnout is *directly caused by work*. It's also important to note that burnout and depression share many of the same symptoms. If you're experiencing any of the symptoms listed above, talk to your doctor or a mental health professional to get the right diagnosis.

So, how do we prevent burnout? We start by looking after ourselves as best we can. We work on our resilience and take care of our mental and physical health. The tips and techniques in this chapter are written to help you prioritise building self-care practices into your working routine. I hope you'll see how this is just as important as making money and growing your business – if not more important.

Bouncing Back

The journalist, public speaker and coach Harriet Minter describes resilience by using the example of running a marathon. 'Endurance is having enough stamina to get around the marathon, even if at the end of it, you fall over,' she says. 'Resilience is pacing yourself well enough that you get around the marathon with a full understanding of what you need to keep going. You know how to stay hydrated; you eat jelly babies and high five people along the way. When you finish the marathon, you still have enough left in the tank so you can walk away.'

Resilience is the ability to recover quickly, a skill anyone who works for themselves needs. If you're resilient, you have the capacity to manage a crisis or a difficult situation and get back to your baseline quickly. In difficult times, it's normal to feel like you lack the resilience to overcome your challenges and you might even tell yourself you're just not built to rebound. But it doesn't have to be this way. The biggest misconception about resilience is that it's a fixed personality trait – it's not, it's a practice. You're not born resilient; anyone can learn how to bounce back. In fact, there are some simple steps you can take to flex your resilience muscle right now.

Dr Lucy Hone, director of the New Zealand Institute of Wellbeing and Resilience and bestselling author, writes about the three strategies for building resilience. The first is acknowledging that suffering is a part of life. Resilient people don't welcome hardships but they do accept that they're a part of life. This helps them not feel like they're a victim of unjust suffering and gives them perspective on their situation.

Second, you need to carefully choose where you're directing your attention. In her research, Dr Hone found that resilient people are able to realistically appraise a situation and can focus on the things they can change and learn to accept those they can't. And lastly, resilience is built when you ask yourself whether what you're doing is helping or harming you. You might ask yourself, 'Is the way I'm thinking or acting helping me or harming me in my bid to land that new client?'

While everyone, regardless of how they work, needs resilience, freelancers face a unique set of challenges that test their emotional durability regularly. When you face rejection on a near-daily basis, it's hard not to take setbacks personally. There's also no one there to remind you to take care of yourself. 'As freelancers, we not only have to think about what we need for our resilience but then we have to make sure we go out and get it ourselves,' Minter tells me. 'Nobody else will provide for us.'

I asked Minter for her three tips for freelancers looking to build resilience:

Rest

Rest is paramount for the simple reason that you can't pour from an empty vessel. We all know we *should* rest but in the throes of feeling overwhelmed, working harder often feels like the only option. But not taking breaks and working late only does you more harm than good in the long run. Instead, aggressively prioritise working reasonable hours and taking time to recharge properly. There's also an important distinction between not working and taking a holiday. When you aren't working because you don't have any work coming in, that's not restful in the slightest. So don't kid yourself into thinking that a week with no work on is the same as a planned and scheduled holiday, even if that break is a staycation. (There's more on how to take holidays later in this chapter.)

The praise folder

Every time someone says something nice about your work, stick it in a folder marked 'Nice things people have said about me'. This can be a folder in your inbox or on your computer. If you like reading things on paper, print the praise out and stick it in a binder. Just make sure you store it in a way that will mean you actually read it next time you have a crisis of confidence.

Feedback loops

We need to feel like we're doing a good job. Start building feedback loops into your systems. This means not only seeking out feedback about your work but then implementing it into your business. This can be as simple as a Google form you send to clients after you complete a project. Minter recommends you do this in such a way as to illicit positive feedback. As well as asking 'what could I do better?' make sure to include questions like 'what did I do well?' or 'what did I do that exceeded expectations?' This way, you'll receive constructive feedback about how to improve your services but also a little confidence boost about what you're already doing brilliantly.

The Loneliest Business

Working in a company of one can be a lonely business. For all of the freedom and flexibility self-employment offers, the risk of isolation is high. If you work alone, either at home or in a workspace, it's easy to go days without any human contact. If you feel lonely working for yourself, know that you're not alone in feeling alone. A 2018 survey from the printer company Epsom found that nearly half (48%) of self-employed workers find it lonely. As counterintuitive as it sounds, loneliness, especially in a work context, isn't always caused by isolation.

According to academic Emma Seppälä, the more people are exhausted by their work, the lonelier they feel. While researching her book, *The Happiness Track*, Seppälä found that loneliness is 'due to the emotional exhaustion of workplace burnout'. Put simply, when you're stressed out and drained by your work, you don't have the energy to interact with others and can easily start to withdraw. The main sign of loneliness is an inability to connect in a meaningful way with others, be that colleagues or family and friends. It can also cause physical symptoms like anxiety, problems sleeping and low energy. In a work context, it leaves you feeling disengaged, less productive and more likely to quit. While Seppälä's research focused on those working in corporate structures, it has applications for freelancers. If anything, suffering from loneliness when you already work alone can make it harder to spot and then to address. Recognising the link between burnout and loneliness, Seppälä suggests that greater human connection at work is needed to solve the problem. For freelancers, this means taking proactive steps to foster deeper social connections, celebrate your wins and work collaboratively. Of course, if your loneliness is due to burnout, you need to address that as well, but here are some tips for easing feelings of isolation:

Sign up for a co-working space

If you miss the buzz of an office and like making new friends, a co-working membership might be right for you. Working outside of your own home may also help create better boundaries around your work. There's more on how to figure out if signing up to a co-working or shared office space is right for you on page 212.

Ad hoc co-working hubs

If you don't want to splurge on a co-working membership, start an informal one of your own. I'm part of a co-working hub with three other freelance writers. We meet up on an ad hoc basic in coffee shops and sometimes in each other's kitchen for a co-working session. These meetups are a lifeline for me because they give me a space to discuss work issues with people I trust and who get what it's like to work for yourself. Even though I tend to get less work done on days I meet with my freelance buddies, I go home feeling supported and re-energised.

Work on site

If you're working on a longer client project and the opportunity to work on site arises, consider taking it. Many freelancers prefer working at home but breaking up the week with a day or two in someone else's office can do wonders for combating loneliness.

Collaborate with other freelancers

Even if you're working from a coffee shop surrounded by other freelancers, it can sometimes feel just as isolating as working alone at home. Consider buddying up with another freelancer and working on a project together. I make a podcast with a good friend of mine and working on it makes me feel like I'm part of a real team. Your fellow freelancers aren't your competition; they're your colleagues. Teaming up to work with them can help you rekindle your passion for your work if it's been waning lately.

Join an online community

As a freelancer, it's as important to network with peers as it is with potential clients. There are plenty of Facebook,

Slack and WhatsApp groups for and by freelancers, as well as physical meetups in local areas. These contacts can lead to potential collaborations or it might just mean you get to know someone with whom you can meet up for a coffee and compare notes. I've met people through online groups who've gone on to become real-life friends. Joining a community is also a great way to build meaningful connections with others who understand what you're going through. There's a list of groups to join on page 304.

Boundaries

In an episode of Brené Brown's *Unlocking Us* podcast, the University of Houston research professor interviews Glennon Doyle about her memoir *Untamed: Stop pleasing, start living*. The pair are talking about boundaries and Brown says, 'People think boundaries are a wall or moat around your heart, but they're not. Good boundaries are a draw-bridge to self-respect.'

In other words, boundaries are about behaviours, not people. I love this distinction because it removes the guilt many of us have when setting our boundaries. Thinking of boundaries as related to behaviours means we don't have to completely cut out the friend who doesn't respect our working hours but rather we can give ourselves permission to limit their behaviour.

The difficulty with boundaries is first we have to work out what they are, then we have to set them and *then* we must actually maintain them. You might already have an intrinsic sense of which behaviours you find unacceptable and want to put a boundary against. If you struggle to identify your boundaries, use these sentences as guidelines to help you figure yours out.

Fill in the blanks:

- People may not _____ (*E.g. People may not undermine my professional experience*)
- I have a right to ask for _____ (*E.g. I have a right to ask for timely payment*)
- It's OK for me to _____ (*E.g. It's OK for me to protect my time by returning emails according to my schedule*)

If you take the time to think about these and jot them down, it will drastically help you maintain your boundaries and you will see an improvement in your working life. It's also important to remember that your boundaries can and will evolve over time. What makes you feel comfortable in one season of your life may make you uncomfortable in another and vice versa. One of my core boundaries is my right to change my mind.

In writing this book, I had to set a lot of boundaries. I actually set aside time to do this; it only took about 20 minutes and made an immeasurable difference not only in the quality of my work but also my stress levels. I knew that in order to complete my draft on time, I needed to carve out two days a week of uninterrupted writing time. This meant setting a boundary with my partner – I asked that he not disturb me when I was at my desk. This was a relatively easy boundary to set. When setting boundaries in a physical space, it can feel more comfortable to use signals, such as a closed door, wearing headphones or sitting in a particular location. This way, you don't have to repeat the boundary every time you want to set it; the headphones will do that for you.

Automate your boundaries

If you struggle to communicate your boundaries in real time, have the robots do it for you instead. I've come to realise that my inbox is my most vulnerable spot, so I like to wrap it in a protective shield of autoreplies and pre-written templates to save myself the mental exhaustion of asking people to respect my time and space. I pretty much have a permanent out-of-office on my emails these days. When I'm on a writing deadline, it says I'm not checking emails at all. Otherwise, my softer, day-to-day autoreply tells recipients that I only check my inbox once a day and that they can expect a reply within three days. I also have a handful of templates saved in my inbox to quickly answer repetitive questions. These include a pre-filled response I send to people who ask me to work for free.

> Hi,
> Thanks so much for your email. This looks super interesting!
>
> For something like this, I'd be more than happy to take this on as a consulting project but unfortunately I can't do it for free. I get a lot of requests like this and I do truly want to help as many people, companies and social enterprises as I can but as a freelancer, I'm at the capacity of the amount of pro bono work I can do.

I have a number of young female journalists whom I mentor and that is what I am concentrating my unpaid work on for the time being.

If you did want me to come on as a consultant, I'd be more than happy to discuss that option.

Thank you for understanding and do keep me in the loop about your project as it does look like a very interesting idea.

Thanks,

Anna

Hi!

Thanks so much for reaching out and for thinking of me.

Unfortunately, I'm currently declining all press/ speaking requests as I'm working on a book at the moment.

Please don't hesitate to contact me again in the autumn and do feel free to check the FAQs on my website in case your questions are answered there.

Thank you!

Anna

Maintaining boundaries takes practice. When I first started using autoreplies in my inbox, I still went into my emails every ten minutes and replied to new messages. But then I realised that if I didn't respect my own boundaries, I could hardly expect others to either. It's no good telling someone you aren't responding to emails to only then go and reply to them instantly.

Breaks and Holidays

How to take a holiday as a freelancer

It was two years before I managed to take a proper holiday as a freelancer. What I mean by proper holiday is going away for two weeks without my laptop. Before that trip, whenever I took time off, I always ended up working during it or only taking a couple of days off. Inevitably, this left me feeling unrested and frustrated and in need of another holiday when I got back. After making this mistake enough times, I've now devised the following strategy for taking time off.

Book your holiday time like it's annual leave

When you work for yourself you effectively have unlimited holiday days. And like any startup employee will tell you, unlimited holidays are great in theory but usually result in you taking less time off than someone with a set amount of vacation time.

It's a good idea to plan your time off well in advance by mapping out roughly how many days you want to take off over the year. From there, block out roughly when you want to take this time off – you don't actually have to book your holiday but having a hold in your diary will remind you when you're taking on a new project that actually, no, you're not available in the second week of September.

Budget for the freelancer holiday tax

Going on holiday is especially painful for freelancers because, in effect, you pay a freelancer holiday tax. By this I mean that on top of the cost of the holiday, you forfeit the money you could have earned had you stayed at home. (This is the dreaded freelance trap in action!) It's a really bad idea to dwell too much on this, though. The best way is instead to try to embrace it as part of the deal and work it into your yearly budget. Put a bit of cash aside each month so that when you do take your holiday, it won't hurt your finances.

Do a pre-flight checklist

Once you have the holiday booked, start getting your ducks in row to ensure you can actually relax while you're there. Make a list that includes what needs finishing before you go; what needs scheduling; who needs to be told you're going away and what needs to be followed up on when you come back. In the run-up to leaving for a vacation, it's vital you prioritise ruthlessly so you can get the urgent and important tasks off your plate and park the ones that can wait until you're back.

Tell your clients

It's not a great idea to hand in a project the day before you go on holiday and then disappear for two weeks. Clients also shouldn't be finding out about your vacation time from your out-of-office. Give them plenty of advance notice that you're going away. Just as you would tell your boss in good time that you're booking time off, you need to tell the people you're freelancing for that you'll be out of action. Don't be worried that they'll be mad at you – they will be a lot madder if you don't tell them and they try to reach you and can't.

Set a clear out-of-office

If your intention is not to look at your emails at all (which it should be if you're on holiday!) then say that in your auto-reply. When I take time off, I write that I am away and not checking emails at all until the date of my return. I say that if someone has a true emergency, they can WhatsApp me. But I don't provide the number because, guess what – if someone has an actual emergency but doesn't have my number, I'm not the person they should be contacting.

Book in work for when you get back

Coming back from holiday with nothing but a credit card bill and no work on the horizon is a sure-fire way of instantly reversing the positive effects of going away in the first place. Before you leave, plan ahead and line up some work that will start when you come back. If you want to get away from feeling like your work is entirely dependent on you being physically present to carry it out, launch an income stream that will continue to bring in money even if you're not there. There's more on how to diversify your income and scaling up your business in chapter five.

Leave your laptop at home

The only way to take a proper holiday is to leave the laptop at home. Don't kid yourself that you're just bringing it to watch Netflix in the evenings – that's a slippery slope and soon enough you'll be replying to emails or thinking that you can 'just do this one thing' because you have your computer with you. If you are organised and prepared before you leave, there really will be no reason to bring it with you.

The virtual commute

Something lots of freelancers who work in their own homes struggle with is finding a way to delineate the end of their working day. When don't leave your office and head home, how do you signal to yourself (and perhaps others you live with) that the work day is over and it's now your time? As I mentioned at the beginning of this chapter, I try to ritualise key moments throughout my day. One of my favourite rituals is my fake commute.

Even though I used to hate commuting when I worked in an office, I did like the feeling of leaving my work behind me by physically going from the office to my house. I now replicate this transition by walking my dogs right after I finish working. It might sound bonkers but in my mind, when I go out with my dogs for a walk, I physically leave my 'office' and come back to my home. Even though it's the same space, it's shifted in my mind. I know a freelancer who does a 'commute' each morning by walking to the coffee shop at the end of her road to buy a coffee.

A virtual commute can also be done without leaving your house. If you used to read a book on the train home from the office, spend 20 minutes at the end of your working day sat in a chair reading instead. When I used to live in a flat with a housemate and I worked from our shared living room, I would mark the end of my working day by packing away my laptop and clearing the table. The kitchen table changed from my desk to the place where we ate dinner. Your ritual should take a form that best suits you.

How to ask for help

At some point, we'll all need to ask for help. Every now and then, it's normal to find yourself with too much on your plate, struggling to cope with something happening in your personal life or stressing about work. Working for yourself doesn't have to mean struggling alone. You *can* ask for help.

It's daunting asking for help and made all the harder when you work alone and don't have an obvious person to approach. Start by trying to figure out what help you actually need. You may be stressed by a large workload and in need of a deadline extension. Your confidence might be down and you could do with some positive feedback and support. Or you might be exhausted from a long stretch of working and in need of a break.

A good first port of call is to talk things through with a trusted freelance friend. Ask them for some time and have a chat. Go into the conversation with an idea of what you need from your friend – whether that's advice or just someone to listen. Also, be explicit with them about what their role is in the discussion; nothing's more infuriating than a housemate trying to give well intentioned career advice when all you wanted was to moan. More often than not, deep down, we know what we need to do in a difficult situation and just the act of sharing that with another person helps immensely.

If the person you need to ask for help is a client, try not to delay too much. The fear of what they'll say may be holding you back but it's better for both of you if you get in touch as soon as you can. As for what to actually say, first start with identifying what outcome you want from the conversation. For example, you might be having a bad mental health moment and need a few extra days to complete a project. Then decide on the most appropriate way to have the conversation, whether that's in person, via phone or email. Whatever the medium, during the conversation clearly explain your situation and what you need. There's no need to be overly apologetic or to go into any details that you don't feel comfortable sharing. Be honest but respect your own boundaries.

For example, if you've been struggling to complete a project because of a mental health problem, you could email something like this:

> *Hi Understanding Client,*
> *I'm sorry to have to do this but I'm going to need a couple more days on the project as I'm experiencing some personal issues at the moment. I can get it over to you by X date.*
> *Thanks for understanding.*

Chapter Summary: Looking After Yourself

Avoid freelancer burnout, build resilience and thrive in your businesses of one with healthy wellbeing practices. The more we learn how to look after ourselves, the healthier our businesses – and we – become.

Resilience can be learned: No one is born resilient; it's a skill that any of us can develop. Accept that setbacks are part of life, learn to realistically appraise a situation and ask yourself whether what you're doing is helping or hindering you. Practise these three things and you'll learn how to bounce back.

Combat loneliness: Working by yourself can be isolating. Combat loneliness by collaborating with other freelancers, joining an online community or working with local freelance friends.

Respect your boundaries: Boundaries are about behaviours, not people. They help you define what you will and won't accept. Define your boundaries, implement them consistently and watch your wellbeing soar.

Rest right: Taking time off isn't a nice-to-have, it's an essential. Plan your breaks, take a virtual commute and learn how to rest properly. You'll have better business results, happier clients and a healthier state of mind.

Ask for help: No matter how good our self-care habits are, bad days are still inevitable. Learn how to ask for help so that when you really need it, the support is there for you.

FREELANCER STORY

Jess B. Cruz (@jessbcruz) – freelance hair colourist

I opened my studio in January 2020 after working for a few years in hair salons in London. I started thinking about working for myself because I was beginning to feel like I was on a conveyor belt. Working in a salon, where you're really overworked, was really stressful. I also felt like I wasn't able to offer the level of service to my clients that I wanted. When I opened my studio, it was really important to me that it became a place where people can actually come and just feel like they're getting one-to-one attention from me.

I never wanted to own a salon with staff and overheads. I wanted to run a small, manageable studio space. I had a vision of a creative place, where I could work and then also rent the space out to other creatives so they could have the potential to earn money from their skills and trade. In my early twenties, I was working long hours in hair salons, getting paid less than minimum wage and sofa surfing. Now I'm in a place where I can potentially give someone a job and pay them a good wage for it. It feels really good to be able to give back more and actually be the change in the industry.

When I first launched, my biggest fear was that my clients wouldn't follow me. But things have only gone from strength to strength since starting out on my own. Not only have I had support from my clients and friends but also from the freelance community. As a hair colourist, I don't do all the services you might get in a salon, which I thought would hold me back. But actually, it's been really fab being able to share clients with other freelancers. We all support each other by recommending one another and there's a real community feeling among the independent and freelance salons and studios. That support helped my confidence grow massively. I jumped in the deep end and just went for it, surprising myself with how capable I've been to pull this together.

Working in this way has opened my eyes to how special independent work is. I now seek out more independent brands and shops myself because I want to support someone who's gone solo. I'm happier paying more for that than I am to give the money to a corporate because I see it as an investment in someone's creativity, just like the investment my clients made in me. I want to be able to give back to the freelance community.

CHAPTER NINE

Working from Anywhere

Of all the things I had to get used to when I went freelance, working from home wasn't one of them. As an introverted only child, I've always been happier in my own company than in that of others. When I worked in-house, I would often try to work from home as much as I could convince my boss to let me. I wanted to write uninterrupted from my empty flat, to pad around in my slippers, a hoody and leggings, making endless cups of tea, as I knew this was how I worked best. Instead, I battled commuter crowds, overheating in my jumper and puffer jacket, only to get to the office flustered and in a bad mood. I'd struggle to get anything done under the glare of strip lighting; I'd stick noise-cancelling headphones on, often without any music playing, to try to drown out the din of the open-plan office. Whenever I had the rare opportunity to work from home, usually under the guise of needing to let in a repair person, it was the bliss I'd imagined it would be.

I assumed that going freelance would mean always operating at this high level of productivity. For the most part, that's been true and I wake up most mornings feeling like I've cheated the system because I no longer have to go into an office. But while working from home has lived up to my expectations, I've also learned many unexpected lessons about productivity when your house doubles up as your office. For starters, I had no idea that laundry, a once loathed task, could suddenly become such an alluring way to procrastinate. I've also experienced how lonely working at home can be when I've held the cashier at the post office in a conversation for too long because they were the only other human I'd spoken to in days.

When I started freelancing, working from home was the exception rather than the rule. But now, because of the pandemic, most people have some experience of it, whether from their own stint of remote work or through living with someone who does it. Working remotely for an employer and working for yourself from home, however, aren't the same thing. You still follow the corporate timetable when you're remote working. This became apparent to me when I started working for myself from home full-time and realised how many bad habits I'd picked up from office life. When I started freelancing, I defaulted to a pattern that mirrored that which I already knew. I got up at roughly the same time I did when I went into an office and worked within the same hours. If I finished all my work by mid-afternoon, which often happened because it's amazing how productive you can be when no one is hassling you, I still sat in my chair until 6pm. If I took 'too long' at lunchtime running an errand, I felt guilty.

After a while, I slowly started tweaking my routine to allow me to work in tune with my natural energy levels. I now often do an hour's work straight after I wake up, in what I call my productivity golden hour. It's when I'm at my peak creative – first thing in the morning, right after a cup of tea, when my phone is still on airplane mode and before I've let the outside world in. It's a very small window I have to be at my most creative and by the time I've showered and let my mind wander too much, the window closes.

In this chapter, I'm going to cover how to figure out when your golden hour is and how to work productively from home. I'll also cover whether it makes sense to upgrade to an external workspace and how to take your work on the road.

In this chapter, you'll learn:

- How to set up a working space on a budget
- What you need to work well from home
- Productivity tips for getting more done
- How to pick a co-working membership

The Home Office

How to set up a home office on a budget

When I first went freelance, I shared a flat with a (non-freelance) housemate. My workspace was the kitchen table in our communal open-plan kitchen/living room. After the first few months of sitting at the dining chair hunched over my laptop, I bought a second-hand office chair which I covered with a blanket to make it look less unsightly. I then went on Amazon and bought a cheap laptop stand, keyboard and mouse to take the pressure off my back. I'd set up my little workstation each morning and pack it up at the end of every day, wanting to be respectful of my flatmate who, understandably, didn't want our table turned into a permanent desk. When you start freelancing, especially if you live in a flat in a major city, you may not have an obvious place to set up as a workspace in your home. Unlike when you were at school or university, you probably don't have a desk in your room. Depending on where you live, your living room – let alone your bedroom – might not even be big enough to fit a desk. You definitely don't need a full room to be your home office but you do need a dedicated space to work. It doesn't have to be big, or even permanent, but you need a spot where you can work comfortably whenever you need to.

If you have a spare room, the obvious solution is to turn it into an office. Most people who have spare rooms use them for guest bedrooms, despite rarely ever hosting over-night stays. Swap the bed for a sofa bed and there will be plenty of space for a desk. The big advantage of a home office is being able to have a proper set-up that's completely separate from your living quarters. A desk, chair and monitor that you don't have to pack away each evening and can shut the door on after you're done working is such a luxury but also an investment in your productivity. If you have to work in a communal area or your bedroom, get creative with the space that you have. I know a freelance writer who built herself a makeshift foldable desk in her cupboard. Is there a nook or cranny you can convert into a small workstation? If your work mainly involves being at the computer, all you need is a space big enough to fit a small laptop. There are plenty of tiny desks that don't take up that much space and can be tucked into a corner or in an unassuming hallway. The kitchen table is also a good solution and one that doesn't require any additional work to get up and running. If you can, consider buying an office chair. Ikea and Made.com have a few affordable, more stylish options than traditional office chairs. If you want a fancy ergonomic chair without the price tag, there are specialist second-hand office furniture suppliers where you can pick up great bargains.

How to set boundaries when you share your workspace

Unless you live alone, or you have a room that you can use as a dedicated office, you'll have to navigate sharing your workspace with the other people who also live in your home. Just because you are at home all day that doesn't mean you should be the one who always waits for the repair person, nor should you be expected to be around to sign for deliveries. It's important to set clear boundaries about your workspace, otherwise it's very easy to become the parcel accepter, housekeeper and childminder just by virtue of working from home.

If you live with people who work outside of the home, especially if they're in a very different line of work from you, it's important to have an open conversation with them about respectfully sharing communal spaces. They may have no idea about the realities of working from home full-time so don't realise that dealing with a handyperson is actually super disruptive to your day. Think about what you want to discuss in advance. Maybe even make some notes. What do you need from them to make sure you can work in peace? For example, you might be happy to accept their deliveries as long as they've asked in advance if you'll be home. If they sometimes work from home as well, perhaps you need a heads up in case you decide to work from somewhere else that day. If the person is also at home during the day, communicate when your working hours are and if you mind being interrupted during them. The people you share with shouldn't take advantage of you but, in return, you also need to respect that the communal areas are not exclusively for your use. Your housemates might not appreciate coming home after work to find a stack of unwashed dishes from your breakfast, lunch and snacks piled in the sink. They might find it appropriate if you made an extra contribution to the utility bills for the extra hours you're running your computer and turning the heating on in the daytime. If you work late into the evening, they might not want you disturbing them watching *Love Island* by taking a work call in the living room.

If you live and work with your partner, you might have an inverse problem to the rest of the coupled population. You spend *too much* time with your other half. Whereas other couples need to make sure they spend enough time together, you need to make sure you have some time apart. At the same time, it's important to still make couple time – seeing each other all day every day while you're working doesn't mean you're spending quality time together so make sure you're still going on date nights regularly.

People who work in offices don't have to think about making sure they're regularly interacting with others but freelancers do. This is especially true for those who live on their own and also work from home. It's all too easy to accidentally go for days without having any human contact, or in the winter without leaving the house at all. The thing about loneliness is that it creeps up on you. Even if you're a homebody who loves your own company and works better alone, too much solitude will get the better of you. You don't necessarily have to join a co-working space but it's a good idea to make a regular habit of getting out of the house. When you do, make sure it's not just popping to the corner shop but rather having meaningful interactions with others. Dinner and drinks with friends in the evening, meetups with fellow freelancers or local community events are all great for the freelance soul.

How to get stuff done at home

When you start working from home, especially if you've been used to working in an office all your professional life, it takes time to adjust. On the one hand, you don't have to commute anywhere and can work in peace from the comfort of your own home. On the other hand, it's easy to get distracted by other tasks around the house and without the pressure of other people around them, many freelancers struggle to be productive. That's why figuring out how you work best and building your working environment around that will help ensure you actually get stuff done at home.

Figure out how you work best

I'm a huge fan of personality tests and quizzes. And not just the ones on Buzzfeed that tell you which *Friends* character you are (Rachel Green, in case you were wondering) but those that actually tell you something useful about yourself.

One of my personal favourite quizzes is Gretchen Rubin's Four Tendencies. In her book of the same name, Rubin outlines four different personality types, depending on how you respond to inner and outer expectations. Inner expectations are personal promises, such as a commitment to start exercising or a New Year's resolution, whereas outer expectations are external, like work deadlines or replying to a request. As such, it's a narrow enough framework that it doesn't veer into making too wide a generalisation about your entire personality. And unlike other personality tests, it's very quick to take and the results will help you understand a lot about yourself, particularly in a work context.

There are four categories: questioners, obligers, upholders and rebels. Which category you fall into depends on how readily you meet inner and outer expectations. For example, I'm a 'questioner', which means I easily meet inner expectations but resist outer ones. I struggle to do things just because someone else told me to, which explains why I prefer working for myself than for others. It also means I can hold myself to account fairly easily, so working from home comes quite naturally to me. By contrast, an 'obliger' readily meets outer expectations but resists inner ones. Obligers, who are the largest category, struggle to hold themselves to account so need an external system like an accountability buddy to check in with their progress. So, if you're an obliger struggling to get stuff done at home, you might find joining a co-working space or an online community of freelancers will help keep you accountable.

Of course, you don't need a personality test to figure out how you like to work; chances are you already have a good idea. Ultimately, it's about an honest evaluation of what you are good and bad at, what distracts you and what conditions you need to do your best work. Knowing this, and honouring it, will help you stay on track.

Get into a routine

Being a freelancer doesn't mean having no routine; it means being able to set one that actually works for you. Many people who struggled in offices because they couldn't cope with early starts find that they can flourish as freelancers because they can shape their days to suit them. It's fine if you want to get up late; just own that decision and adjust your routine around it. A regular schedule with defined working hours might sound stuffy and restrictive but it actually gives you the freedom to clearly delineate between work and play. This doesn't have to mean a fixed 9 to 5, but maybe you'll only take calls in the afternoon, and leave your mornings for creative work. Or maybe you allow yourself some flexibility around when you start work – everyone has a different ideal start time. I like to think that the best schedules fit you like your favourite pair of jeans. They're comfortable and reliable but there's wriggle room in them. Your schedule shouldn't be packed in so tight that if something slips, everything falls apart.

Off-peak hours

And finally, what's the point of being freelance if you don't clock off and go to the movies in the afternoon once in a while? I'm not kidding. If you can work flexibly, make sure you do actually work flexibly. If you finish a project earlier than anticipated, there's no need to sit at your desk for the sake of it – take the rest of the day off. If it's a beautiful day outside, go for a walk at lunchtime. Don't feel guilty about this! You might not have a free dental plan or corporate gym membership but this is by far one of the best perks of the job. Also, make sure to take advantage of being able to set your own schedule and opt for off-peak options whenever you can. During the daytime, not only is it quieter, but there's also a whole world of discounts only available to those with flexible schedules. Not only is travel cheaper outside of rush hour, but gyms, hotels and even hairdressers offer off-peak rates.

The Productive Freelancer

The art of productivity can be learned. I believe that when it comes to productivity, it's easier to just follow a tried-and-tested method than to start one from scratch. The following are productivity techniques I've found especially helpful for keeping me focused and getting stuff done as a freelancer. You don't have to do them all and you definitely don't have to do them all at the same time. Not all of them will appeal to you and that's OK. Just keep an open mind and try the ones that sound like a good fit.

The Pomodoro Technique

The Pomodoro Technique is a very simple trick for doing uninterrupted, focused work. You pick a task and set a timer for 25 minutes and work only on that task until the timer rings. After your timer is up, you take a five-minute break. If your task was computer-based, it's a good idea to also take a screen break. Rinse and repeat another three times and then take a longer break of up to half an hour. It took me actually giving this a try to realise just how much work you can get done when you focus on one task at a time. The Pomodoro Technique works really well for a number of different types of tasks. I personally like to use it for writing (in fact, I'm doing it right now). Others find it more useful for doing boring admin tasks. It's also a great hack to use when you're struggling to start a project that you keep putting off or that feels too big to start. Setting a timer for 25 minutes gives you a manageable framework to just begin.

Calendar blocking

This method sees you take the things you've written on your to-do list (or your can-do list!) and convert them into blocks of time in your calendar. Every task you have to do effectively becomes an appointment in your diary. The advantage of calendar blocking is that you commit time to the tasks you need to do. It helps you develop a better sense of how long it actually takes you to complete a task because when you assign a specific slot to it, it makes you take action. Just as you would schedule a call or an out-of-office appointment, start scheduling tasks like 'invoice client and record weekly expenses', 'plan social media posts' and 'email client back'. So many of us are guilty of overloading our to-do lists. Calendar blocking is particularly helpful for anyone who hates the disappointment of coming to the end of a day and not being able to tick everything off their list.

The Ivy Lee method

In 1918, the American steel tycoon Charles M. Schwab hired a prominent businessman named Ivy Lee to improve his company's efficiency. Lee came up with a very simple method for the company executives to follow: at the end of each working day, write down the six most important tasks that need to get done the next day and number them in order of importance. The next morning, start working on the first task and don't move on to the second one until it's completed. If you get to the end of the day and haven't finished everything on the list, just keeping going the next day.

The simple time management tool is still recommended today by some of the world's leading productivity experts, including James Clear, the author of *Atomic Habits*. The method is very good for people who have a lot of small to medium-sized tasks on their plate and who struggle to focus on important tasks over urgent ones. It also pairs well with the Pomodoro Technique as you can work on your tasks in 25-minute chunks.

Eat the Frog

Mark Twain is believed to have said, 'If it's your job to eat a frog, it's best to do it First Thing in the Morning. And if it's your job to eat two frogs, it's best to eat the BIGGEST one first.' This idea of beating procrastination by doing the hardest task first was then popularised by the self-development author Brian Tracy in his bestselling book *Eat That Frog!*

Eating the frog means starting your day by tackling your biggest, most important task first. This is the one thing that will have the biggest impact on your day, or even career, but it often happens to be the one you're most likely to procrastinate on. In order to figure out what the 'frogs' in your working life are, Tracy developed a system for prioritising your work. It's similar to the Ivy Lee method but goes into more depth about the nature of your tasks. Rather than number your to-do list in order of importance, you order the items on it by type of task and assign them a letter A, B, C, D or E:

- 'A' tasks are things that must be done. Examples of A tasks include fulfilling customer orders or meeting a client deadline.
- 'B' tasks are things you should do. These include checking your emails or returning unimportant calls. Someone may be inconvenienced if you don't do these tasks but the consequences are not dire.

- 'C' tasks are those that are nice to do but have no consequences. These include going for lunch with a fellow freelancer or attending a networking event.
- 'D' tasks are those that can be delegated. These are things that can be done by someone else or automated. Transcribing audio files is a good example of a 'D' task.
- 'E' tasks need to be eliminated. You may find a task becomes an E if it was once important but your plans changed and it's now no longer a priority.

By grouping your tasks by their importance, you'll put your focus where it's really needed. This method is particularly useful for anyone prone to procrastination and who otherwise tends to tick off the easier items on their to-do lists before the real priorities.

Bullet journaling

Have you bought diaries, planners and journals only to abandon them a few weeks later because they were not quite right? A bullet journal (also known as a 'bujo') might be for you. Made popular by Instagram posts of beautiful weekly spreads, bujos are a DIY planner-calendar-notebook hybrid. Described as 'the analogue method for the digital age', it was invented by the digital product designer Ryder Carroll. The idea is to take notes in a way that works for you. You could use a bullet journal to put some of the previous productivity methods together, such as calendar blocking and the Ivy Lee Method. You can also capture inspirational quotes in your bujo, right alongside your client meeting notes.

Bullet journals work best for anyone who likes to write by hand and those who prefer paper calendars to digital ones. They also work great for creative types who want their planners to double up as works of art. The official bullet journal recommendation is to use a dotted notebook with page numbers and an index but any old notebook will do. For the full instructions for setting up a bullet journal and getting started, visit www.bulletjournal.com

Upgrading to an Office

Do you need a co-working membership?

Many freelancers leave their staff jobs behind because they have an allergy to offices and don't look back. However, there are plenty of freelancers who miss working in offices. We are, after all, social creatures who want to be around others.

If you're really struggling to get work done at home and finding it too isolating, you might want to consider joining a co-working space. Originally designed for tech startups, the latest slew that have popped up in the last few years are specifically geared towards freelancers and independent workers. This is reflected in the pricing, as some offer plans that allow you to pay as you go, rather than committing you to a year's membership. The advantages of a co-working space include having access to a proper workstation and other office-like features, such as printing and meeting rooms. Lots of co-working spaces also offer community benefits like events and networking opportunities. If you're thinking of joining one, here's what you need to consider.

What are the membership options?

Most co-working spaces offer three tiers of membership. The cheapest is a hot desk plan, which gives you access to a shared workspace and you grab a free spot where you can. The second tier is a fixed desk – this usually includes a proper chair and a lockable filing cabinet you can leave your things in. Unlike with a hot desk, you can leave your things behind if you have a fixed desk. The most expensive option is a private office. This is usually a small cabin or space within the co-working building that's lockable and can fit in a number of desks. Each co-working space offers different amenities, like postal handling and meeting room hire, either included in the price as standard or at an additional cost. Shop around and compare membership offerings before signing on the dotted line.

Is the price right?

The cost of co-working varies greatly, ranging from £100 a year to £500 a month depending on the venue and type of membership. While you can expense the membership cost on your tax return that's not reason enough to pick the fanciest place, just because the loos are Instagrammable.

Location, location, location

If the co-working space you have your eye on is on the other side of town and you hate commuting in rush hour, the chances of you actually going are slim. Think not just about your current location but if you're planning on moving anytime soon or if you travel a lot for work. Some of the larger co-working companies have international locations, or even just different sites around town that you can use between meetings.

Do you like the vibe?

Probably the most important factor to consider when choosing a workspace is your gut feeling when you visit it. Each space has its own culture and personality; some are populated by twenty-somethings with man buns while others are filled with social enterprises just starting out. Factors like noise levels, ambient music, temperature and even the coffee situation are deeply personal choices so think about these as you're making your decision. Most co-working spaces will let you take a tour before signing up, which you should definitely take advantage of – also make sure to read the fine print before signing up, especially regarding cancelation terms. This is going to be your place of work for the foreseeable future, so make sure you get a good sense of the place before committing to it.

But can you print?

If one of the reasons you want a co-working membership is because you can't (or don't want to) turn your living room into an office then make sure the venue actually offers the facilities you need. Do you want a space with a proper office chair? Do you need access to a meeting room? What are the printing facilities like? Don't get side-tracked by the free coffee and swanky gym if the amenities you actually need aren't there.

To Co-work or Not?

Why you should join a co-working space:

- You can afford it
- You're in a line of work, like consulting or coaching, that requires regular in-person meetings
- It's impossible to work where you live
- You work better around others
- It offers facilities or services you actually need

Why you shouldn't join a co-working space:

- To post pictures of it on Instagram
- You can't afford it
- It's too far from your house or you don't like to commute

Should I rent an office?

If you're considering renting a dedicated workspace or a hot desk, co-working membership will probably do you just fine. There are, however, particular situations in which you might want to consider renting a private office. You can rent a private space within a co-working space, which will also give you access to the communal benefits of a co-working membership – this works well for freelancers who need a place where they can close the door but would like to also be part of a community. Alternatively, you can rent directly from a commercial landlord – this suits freelancers who need specialist equipment or have more complex business needs. Here are a few situations in which you may want to consider renting a private workspace.

You want to look professional

Freelancers who work in the professional or financial services sector, like accountants, management consultants and financial advisors, may want to meet clients in their own office rather than a coffee shop. It just looks more professional, especially to clients who are coming to you for private or delicate matters.

You need a lot of space

A studio is basically an office for artists. Creative freelancers, like painters, fashion designers and musicians, might need to rent a studio to store their materials, tools and instruments. Studios will generally have better lighting than you'll get at home or in a co-working space. You may also want to consider a private office or studio if you carry stock – like craftspeople who make items to sell on to their customers.

You need specialist kit

If you make a lot of video calls or need ultra-high-speed internet, office rentals will offer better options than you can get at home. Some lines of work, like freelance hair stylists, makeup artists and beauticians, also need specialist equipment. If you've leased your private office directly from the landlord, you'll also have more control over the layout and interior design. You'll be able to bring in any specific signage or furniture you need.

You have team members

Not all freelancers work alone. Some have assistants or regularly employ other freelancers to help them on projects and need a space where they can all work together.

The World Is Your Workplace

Freelancing outside major cities

There's no rule that says you have to freelance from a major city. I always thought I was a Londoner through and through but once I started working for myself, I realised I could be happier outside of the metropolis and moved out.

In the last few years, rural freelancing has been on the rise. Now, twice as many of the 4.8 million self-employed people in the UK live in towns, villages and hamlets compared with cities, according to Modern Working Mag. Some rural areas, like St Ives in Cornwall and Dwyfor Meirionnydd in Wales, have vibrant freelance communities where the self-employed workforce is more than double that of the national average. Thanks to advances in digital communication tools and the rise of remote working, gone are the days when you needed to live in the same city – or indeed country – as your clients. Instead, you can often base your decision on where to live on factors like quality of life, proximity to family and cost of living.

Of course some industries are more suited to remote working. As the industry that pioneered it, anything tech-related translates well to working remotely. Journalists and bloggers also fare well outside of cities. For any writer, it can be an advantage to move somewhere underrepresented and own that beat. Depending on your line of work, moving outside of a major city can also offer a competitive advantage. If you have an in-demand skill, relocating somewhere where it's in low supply would be a smart move. There are also a number of local authorities who offer grants to freelancers and small businesses to attract them to work in their region.

Digital nomads

Freedom of how you work extends to where you work. The idealised Instagram image of the modern freelancer is of someone sat by the pool with their laptop. While what you see on social media is an exaggeration, it is *almost* true that you can work from anywhere, so long as you have a stable and secure internet connection.

In the last few years, the term 'digital nomad' has exploded in popularity. A digital nomad is someone who travels the world while working remotely. They are basically a free-lancer constantly on the move. It's not a lifestyle for everyone but if you love travelling, have an adventurous spirit and are comfortable with uncertainty then you might be cut out for being a digital nomad. There are plenty of advantages to this lifestyle, the first of course being that you get to travel and see the world. It's a different sort of travelling from going on holiday; often digital nomads will relocate to a new place for a longer stretch of time, between three months and a year. Depending on where in the world you go, you can significantly lower your cost of living. Berlin, Athens, Bali and Bangkok are all popular destinations for digital nomads because they offer a cheaper, less hectic life.

Anyone whose work doesn't require them to be physically present somewhere can be a digital nomad, from writers and designers to online marketers and consultants. All you need is a laptop, an internet connection and an appetite for adventure to make it work. If you think that combining work with travel might be for you, here are some things to consider.

Cut your location ties

For many entry-level freelancers, the only real tie they have to a place is their tenancy agreement. If you're serious about giving the digital nomadic lifestyle a go, the first place to start is by cutting the financial cords that are keeping you in your current location. Flat leases, phone contracts and gym memberships need to go as you transition into a pay-as-you-go set-up.

Navigate the international tax system

A big administrative headache for digital nomads is tax. You'll need to figure out which countries you're liable to pay tax in. As far as UK tax is concerned, you'll still be considered a UK tax resident if you spend 183 days in the UK each year. As for paying tax abroad, that will depend on the country's tax policy and how much time you spend there. If you're planning to move around a lot for work, speak to an accountant to make sure your tax affairs are in order.

Join a remote work programme

A way to ease into the digital nomadic life is by doing a remote work programme. Companies like Remote Year and Hacker Paradise offer organised around-the-world trips specifically for professionals who want to work while travelling. All your accommodation and travel will be taken care of so you can focus on enjoying your trip. As long as you meet the programme's requirements, which are usually that you need to be over 21, a fluent English speaker and able to support yourself financially, freelancers are welcome on these tours.

Find remote part-time work

Whether you move around or stay put, anchor clients can be a lifeline for freelancers. Anchor clients are those who provide regular work on an ongoing basis which you know you can rely on each month. If you can do this work remotely, when you hit the road you'll be doing so knowing that you have a reliable pay cheque each month. And if that client is in an expensive city, paying you local wages, they will go a lot further if you travel to destinations with a lower cost of living, like Asia and Eastern Europe.

Chapter Summary: Working from Anywhere

Learn how to be productive while working from home and upgrade your working space when you're ready.

The productive freelancer: From calendar blocking and the Ivy Lee Method to the Pomodoro Technique, finding a productivity hack that works for you will boost your efficiency.

Home office life: Set up a dedicated space that you can work from comfortably, prioritising your back health and your boundaries.

When to co-work: Co-working spaces are great if you need the buzz of other people to keep you motivated.

Remember to be flexible: Don't forget to take advantage of being the master of your own schedule. Go to the movies in the daytime every now and then.

Digital nomads: If you want to combine travel with your work, cut your financial ties and take your work on the road

---

FREELANCER STORY

Sapphire Bates (@thecovengirlgang) – founder of The Coven Girl Gang

I was in Thailand, in my early twenties, when I decided to become self-employed. I'd been kicked out of sixth form, I didn't go to university and I was starting to run out of money. I didn't have a plan but I knew what I didn't want to do. I'd had my first taste of freedom and not having anybody tell me what to do. I couldn't imagine going back and working for somebody else. And so I found myself sitting in an internet cafe in northern Thailand, Skyping with my mum and brainstorming ideas of what my future was going to look like. In the end, it came down to taking a teaching job in China or starting my own business. I was actually more keen on the teaching idea but it was my mum who encouraged me to give self-employment a go.

I ended up starting a floristry business because that was the only experience I had, having qualified as a junior florist.

I was by no means ready; I had no real idea about ordering flowers, doing accounts or how to even become self-employed. But I just decided I'd give it a go. I said to myself that I'd try it for a year and see if I could make enough money to pay the bills. I ran my floristry business for a couple of years. I also did freelance floristry for other big companies because I made quite good money from that. It was going well but my income was still very sporadic.

It was when I got the opportunity to move abroad again that I started thinking about how I could start an online business that would allow me to travel while I worked. I ended up stumbling on the idea for The Coven. One of the things I came across on my own journey of work was a lot of isolation. I was just by myself. I didn't have any staff, I spent all my time alone and I found it really isolating, and I started to realise that other people did too. The idea was to start a digital membership community with its sole aim being to provide a support network for freelancers and founders. Just like with the floristry business, I bootstrapped the idea and ran with it. The launch went even better than I could have hoped for. I ended up closing my floristry business after two months and I've been working online doing that ever since.

When I look back over my career, everything I've done has been the result of what life's thrown at me. I feel really fortunate that the thing I've wanted to do worked. Everything I've done has always been driven by the life I wanted to create for myself, be that wanting to live abroad or be in charge of my own hours. It's always been about fitting my work around my life as opposed to having my life fit around my career.

CHAPTER TEN

Freelancing and Families

Around the time I went freelance, I started thinking I might be ready to buy my first home. By that point, I'd moved around rentals for the best part of ten years and I wanted to nest in my own place. As any millennial will tell you, home ownership already felt like an impossible dream. The statistic that one in three millennials will never own a home rang in my ears. And then I actually tried to buy a home as a self-employed person. Even if you've managed to save enough for a deposit, lenders want to see a lot more evidence of your finances than they do for employees, typically asking for a minimum of two years' worth of documentation.

After all the hoops I jumped through, it's taken me over three years to get to a point where buying a house might just be a reality. As I'm writing this now, I've had an offer accepted and I'm in the thick of the buying process. Buying a house is stressful at the best of times and I happened to buy mine in the middle of a pandemic. To make matters worse, I applied for a joint mortgage with my partner and experienced first-hand the sting of how self-employed people are treated compared to our staff counterparts. I had to show three years of tax returns and six months' worth of bank statements on top of all the usual documents, while my partner only needed one payslip. In the end, a freelance friend recommended a mortgage broker who specialised in self-employed applications who guided me through the process and helped me get everything in order.

The greatest joy of self-employment is the freedom to build a life that works for you, one that accommodates your life plans rather than the other way around. While it's a working style that makes most of us who chose this path happy (and therefore more productive), social infrastructure hasn't caught up yet. Running a business of one can feel like the most grown-up thing you've ever done and then you find yourself unable to enjoy the milestones other adults take for granted. As I found when I tried to apply for a mortgage, mainstream social and economic systems aren't designed for us.

In my first years of freelancing, when I knew I wanted to buy a house soon, I had to make some tough calls. As I applied for a joint mortgage with a partner, there was the option to not even put my self-employed income down and only apply in my partner's name. I wasn't prepared to do that because I felt, as a woman who's worked hard to build her self-employed empire these last few years, that would betray my principles. I also made business decisions that I knew would look good for my mortgage application but weren't always ideal for my business. I shied away from taking risks because I wanted to make sure my profits remained steady and reliable. This turned out to be important because mortgage providers lend to you based on your profits rather than your turnover. So, in order to maximise the amount I could borrow, I showed higher profits by declaring fewer business expenses than I was entitled to and therefore footed a higher tax bill. You might feel less comfortable taking a tax hit than you do applying for a mortgage in your partner's name.

Either way, there are frustrating sacrifices that you'll probably need to make.

This is the one chapter of the book I urge you to read even if you don't think you're quite ready for it. You might not be considering buying a house right now, planning on having a kid or even thinking about retiring, but given the lead time you'll need, it's worth having this information at the back of your mind. Pensions, parental leave and property purchases don't make for sexy dinner party chat. They can also feel scary so we shy away from thinking about the practicalities of them. The problem for freelancers, though, is that reaching these adulting milestones is that much harder for us. In all cases, they require a lot of forward planning. So this chapter might not apply to you right now but it will at some point. And it's good to know the realities of the situation sooner rather than later.

In this chapter, you'll learn:

- What rights you're entitled to as a working parent
- How to buy a house as a self-employed person
- What retirement options are available for freelancers

Parental leave

No matter your employment status, the right to take time off to have a child should be available to all. Unfortunately, that isn't the case, and parental leave is a key area in which self-employed workers suffer greatly. While there are some rights and benefits available to self-employed parents, they aren't comparable with those enjoyed by their employed counterparts.

If you're thinking of having a family, this section will help you wrap your head around what is – and isn't – available to you so that you can plan for the future.

Maternity pay and leave

Expectant mothers who work for an employer are entitled to maternity leave and pay. Self-employed mothers don't have access to this but they may be eligible for Maternity Allowance instead. This is a benefit paid by the Department of Work and Pensions to birth mothers who do not qualify for statutory maternity pay. How much you'll get is dependent on your eligibility. (Note: if you're set up as a limited company, you may still be entitled to statutory maternity pay; details about this can be found later in this section.)

How much Maternity Allowance you can get

The maximum amount you can get is £151.20 a week or 90% of your average weekly earnings (whichever is less) for 39 weeks. It's worth noting that this amount is in line with statutory maternity pay. It's also tax free because it's a state benefit. However, if you don't qualify for the full amount, you'll only receive £27 a week for either 39 or 14 weeks depending on how you qualify.

To get the full amount of Maternity Allowance, you need to have paid Class 2 national insurance contributions for at least 13 of the 66 weeks before your baby's due date. If you haven't paid enough to get the full rate, you'll get the lower rate. It is possible to make extra national insurance contributions to make sure you get the full amount of Maternity

Allowance. When you make your claim, HMRC will tell you how to do this.

How to claim Maternity Allowance

In order to claim Maternity Allowance, you have to complete a form known as the MA1, which you can download online from gov.uk or have sent to you. You cannot claim online. You can find the form here: www.gov.uk/maternity-allowance/how-to-claim

When you claim, you don't need to prove your self-employed earnings as your NI contributions record will get checked. If you aren't sure if you're eligible for Maternity Allowance, make a claim and the Department for Work and Pensions will work out whether you qualify.

If you are not entitled to Maternity Allowance, your application will automatically be checked to see if you can get a different benefit, Employment and Support Allowance (Maternity), which is paid for six weeks before your baby is due until 14 days after the birth. There are also other family benefits you may be entitled to, which are outlined further on in this chapter.

Working while receiving Maternity Allowance

Many new mothers will want to start working again after having their baby. If you're still claiming Maternity Allowance, you can work for up to ten 'keeping-in-touch' (KIT) days without losing it. If you work for more than ten KIT days, you'll lose some or all of your weekly Maternity Allowance payments, depending on how much work you are doing.

The guidelines on working during your Maternity Allowance period consider *any* day in which you work to be a KIT day, regardless of how little you worked. So, if you only did an hour's work, that would count as a whole KIT day. For this reason, it's best to do as much work as possible in one day so as not to use up too many KIT days. You also have to keep a record of the days that you worked otherwise the DWP will make an estimate on your behalf.

As for what counts as 'work', the guidelines say that any work you normally do in the course of your job counts as a KIT day. However, you can carry out minimal maintenance and admin tasks without claiming these as KIT days. These are tasks that need to be done in order to keep your business going for which you don't receive any direct payment. This includes necessary admin; accepting work due to start after your Maternity Allowance ends; essential maintenance to your website or equipment; responding to correspondence requesting information as long as it does not relate to work to be carried out before your Maternity Allowance ends; keeping essential formal qualifications and licences up to date; keeping skills at an acceptable level (this should not include formal paid-for training) and preparing for work arranged before your Maternity Allowance period starts but to be carried out after it ends.

Maternity Action, the UK's leading maternity rights charity, gives the following examples on its website of DWP decisions on working more than ten KIT days:

Jane worked full-time running her own catering business before having her baby. She worked for ten KIT days since having her baby. She wants to continue working one day a week for the next eight weeks. She should only be disqualified from receiving MA for a day a week for those eight weeks. Maternity Allowance can be divided into daily rates where necessary, so she should have one seventh deducted from her weekly Maternity Allowance payment.

Emma worked two days a week as a freelance trainer before having her baby. She has completed ten KIT days since having her baby and has been offered work for two days a week over a five-week period. She may be disqualified from receiving Maternity Allowance for those five weeks as she has returned to her normal working pattern. If Emma stops work during her MA period, she should contact MA Claims and ask for her MA to be reinstated.

Maternity leave for limited company directors

As the director of a limited company, even if you're the only one working in your business, as far as HMRC is concerned, you're an employee. As such, you're entitled to the same maternity leave rights as expectant mothers in large organisations and might be able to claim statutory maternity pay.

If you qualify, statutory maternity pay is paid for up to 39 weeks. It's 90% of your average weekly earnings before tax for the first 6 weeks. After this, it is £148.68 or 90% of your average weekly earnings (whichever is lower) for the next 33 weeks.

You will have to pay your own statutory maternity pay from your limited company and then claim it back from HMRC. In some cases, it's possible to receive advance funds from HMRC if you can't afford to pay yourself. For more information on advance payments of SMP see: www.gov.uk/recover-statutory-payments/if-you-cant-afford-to-make-payments

In order to claim statutory maternity pay, you'll need to meet the following criteria:

- You are considered an employee of your own limited company
- You work for your limited company as an employee in the fifteenth week before your baby is due and have worked for a minimum of 26 weeks before that
- Other workers are able to fulfil your duties while you're on maternity leave
- The company can earn enough money while you're on maternity leave and can afford to pay your statutory maternity pay

If you don't meet these criteria, you'll need to claim Maternity Allowance instead.

Paternity pay and leave

Freelancers who want to take time off when their partners have a baby have no right to any paid leave whatsoever. There's no equivalent of Maternity Allowance for expectant fathers and partners (this includes same-sex partners) who want to take time off. This is also the case for adoption and surrogacy.

The only exception is for expectant fathers and partners who are set up as a limited company. In this case, you may be entitled to statutory paternity pay, which is either £151.20 a week or 90% of your average weekly earnings (whichever is lower) for up to two weeks. Your limited company would fund this and then you can claim it back from HMRC.

Shared parental leave

Shared parental leave allows mothers to end their maternity leave and/or pay early so that one or both parents can take time off in a more flexible way during the baby's first year. But shared parental leave is only available to employees. So, if an expectant mother is self-employed and claiming Maternity Allowance, she is *not* entitled to take shared parental leave or statutory shared parental pay. However, if her partner is employed, they may be entitled to paternity leave and/or shared parental leave.

Fathers or partners who are self-employed are also not able to take shared parental leave or statutory shared parental pay. In cases where both parents are self-employed, the mother can claim Maternity Allowance but cannot transfer any of it to her partner.

The situation for fathers, partners, adoptive and surrogate parents is, quite frankly, an utter travesty. Sufficient paternity leave allows you to support your partner postpartum and bond with your new child, and it fosters gender equality. The brutal reality for expectant fathers and partners is that it's down to you to plan ahead to take time off to have a child. Further on in this section there are details on how to do this.

Other family benefits

Even if you don't qualify for Maternity Allowance, or are on a low income, there are other family benefits you might be entitled to.

Child Benefit

Once your baby is born, you can claim Child Benefit. Payments are tax free as long as neither parent earns more than £50,000 a year. It's important to note that if you're off work looking after your child and not paying national insurance contributions, claiming Child Benefit will ensure you get credits towards your state pension. For more information visit www.gov.uk/child-benefit

Universal Credit

If your family income is reduced because you are taking unpaid time off to look after a new baby or child under three, you may be able to claim Universal Credit. Under Universal Credit rules, if you're claiming Maternity Allowance, it's treated as unearned income and is deducted from a Universal Credit award. For more information visit www.gov.uk/self-employment-and-universal-credit

Sure Start Maternity Grant

If you or your partner are receiving Income Support, income-based Jobseekers Allowance, Universal Credit or Child Tax Credit you may be entitled to a Sure Start Maternity Grant, a one-off payment of £500 for your first child (or if there are no other children aged under 16 in your family) or first multiple birth. You can find out more information at www.gov.uk/sure-start-maternity-grant

Employment Support Allowance

If you are not well enough to work, you may be eligible for New-style (contribution-based) Employment and Support Allowance: www.gov.uk/guidance/new-style-employment-and-support-allowance

Planning ahead

As you'll have gathered by this point, the benefits available to freelance expectant parents are very limited compared to their staff counterparts. If you're planning on having a family as a freelancer and want to take time off, you have to plan ahead. How you do this will depend on a number of factors, such as your family situation; whether your partner is also self-employed or in a staff role; and how your business is set up, whether as a sole trader or limited company.

Start by finding out what you'll be able to claim as an expectant parent. Every situation is different so contact HMRC, the job centre or Citizens Advice for more information. There are contact details in the directory at the back of the book.

It's also important to understand what your partner is entitled to. Depending on whether you're both self-employed or one of you is employed by a company, this will impact what you'll get. For example, while a freelance expectant father (set up as a sole trader) isn't entitled to paternity pay, the employed partner of an expectant self-employed mother will be.

As far as saving goes, start putting money aside to cover your own parental leave as soon as you decide to have a baby. There are savings tips that you can use to build up this pot in the next chapter.

Pensions

A lack of financial education about the benefits of retirement savings and the simple fact that no one *makes* you open a pension have led to 62% of self-employed people currently having no form of pension savings. With no HR department to automatically enrol you into a pension scheme, it's down to you to sort out how you're going to save for your retirement.

Currently, the maximum amount you can get from the state pension is £175.20 a week (or £9,110.40 a year). For most people, this is significantly less than what they'd like to retire on. Put bluntly, don't rely on the state pension alone to see you through your golden years. Instead, see it as one part of your retirement fund, which you have plenty of ways of boosting, as you'll see in this section.

As for how you get a state pension, you need a minimum of ten qualifying years of national insurance contributions. If you want to receive the full amount, you'll need 35 qualifying years of NI contributions.

Before I explain what your options are as far as self-employed pensions go, first I need to talk about compound interest. Academic folklore has it that when asked what mankind's greatest invention was, Albert Einstein replied 'compound interest'. Regardless of whether Einstein actually said this, there's no question that compound interest is a wondrous thing. It's interest you earn on interest. Let's say you have £100, which earns 10% interest a year. At the end of the year, you have your original £100, plus £10 (10% of £100) in interest. The following year, you'll earn 10% interest on that £110, leaving you with £121. After 30 years, your initial £100 will have grown into £1,744.94. Compound interest is what makes your pension pot grow over time, effectively making your money work for you. The interest rate you get in a pension scheme (plus the additional tax benefits I'll explain later) make them a unique kind of savings fund that will pay off in the long run.

Options for self-employed pensions

Your main option for a retirement fund is to open what's known as a personal pension. This is a specifically designed financial product which will help your money grow over time and benefits from tax relief; you can only access this money once you reach retirement age.

There are three types of personal pensions:

Ordinary pension

Also known as a private pension or a defined contribution pension, an ordinary pension is managed for you by your pension provider. Usually this means your money is invested into a pooled fund of stocks and shares. Ordinary pensions are widely offered by most providers.

Self-invested personal pension (SIPP)

A self-invested personal pension (SIPP) is similar to an ordinary pension except that you manage it yourself. This gives you the flexibility to choose which funds to invest in. SIPPs are suitable for people comfortable managing their own investments as you can choose from a wide range of assets to invest in, from stocks and shares to commercial property and trusts.

Stakeholder pension

Stakeholder pensions are popular with those on low incomes and the self-employed because they offer a minimum contribution, have capped charges and you can stop and start your payments. The pot is managed for you, so you don't have to decide where to invest your money. Money from a stakeholder pension can be accessed from the age of 55, which is set to increase to 57 from 2028.

Remember, all private pension schemes are investments and the value of your pension pot can go up or down depending on how the investments perform. As well as personal pensions, you also have the following retirement savings options:

National Employment Savings Trust

The government's National Employment Savings Trust (NEST) can be used by freelancers. You can join if you're self-employed or are the sole director of a company that doesn't employ anyone else. The scheme is run as a trust by the NEST Corporation which means there are no shareholders or owners and it's run for the benefit of its members. To see if you're eligible, check NEST's website: www.nestpensions.org.uk

Lifetime ISA

The Lifetime ISA (Individual Savings Account) is a government-backed scheme specifically designed to help you buy your first house or save for retirement. Most major banks and building societies offer Lifetime ISAs.

You can put up to £4,000 into a Lifetime ISA every tax year and the government then adds a 25% bonus to your savings, up to a maximum of £1,000 a year. You also earn interest on whatever you save, which is tax free because the account is an ISA.

If you use a Lifetime ISA for retirement savings, you can only access the funds after your sixtieth birthday. You don't have to take it all out at once and if you leave money in the Lifetime ISA it will continue to grow interest.

It's important to note that Lifetime ISAs operate differently from personal pensions. For starters, they're taxed differently from pension schemes. A pension is tax free when you pay into it but you're taxed on the money you withdraw from it. A Lifetime ISA is the reverse: you contribute money you've already paid tax on but eligible withdrawals are tax free. Unlike a pension, Lifetime ISA savings will affect your eligibility for benefits.

Martin Lewis, founder of Money Saving Expert, advises that, in most cases, a pension beats a Lifetime ISA as a first place to save for retirement. The exception to this is in the case of sole trader, basic rate taxpayers who may find a Lifetime ISA an attractive option for their retirement fund. It's also possible to have a LISA in addition to a personal pension or NEST scheme.

Saving into a pension as a limited company

If you're set up as a limited company, you can either pay into your pension personally or through your business. Pension contributions are treated as an allowable business expense, meaning your company's corporation tax bill will be lower. It's generally the case that making your contributions through your limited company is more tax efficient than if the same contribution were taken from your own funds, however you should always seek independent financial advice first.

Planning for freelance retirement

It might feel like you're going to have to work for the rest of your life but that doesn't have to be *quite* the case. It's important, however, to be realistic and understand that, as a freelancer, you won't have an employer topping up your pension so you may have to save harder if you want a bountiful retirement.

Most people will start to panic about their pensions in their mid-thirties. They'll go onto an online retirement checker and be shocked when they see how little they've got coming their way. Instead, the trick is to learn enough about pensions so that you don't miss out on key savings but not completely freak yourself out of saving anything at all.

Start by working out a goal for how much you'd ideally want to retire on. This figure will vary for everyone and will depend on your personal circumstances. To give you a rough idea, figures issued by *Which?* in 2020 found that individuals who enjoy a comfortable retirement spend on average £19,000 a year, whereas those who enjoy a luxurious retirement spend £30,000. Factors like where you live, whether you own your home outright and whether you have dependants will all affect this figure so it's important to do this calculation based on your personal circumstances. Go into this understanding that you'll be facing some huge numbers here; if you want to retire on £30,000 a year at 60 and expect to live until you're 90, that's nearly £1 million. Don't get spooked by this; instead focus on the steps you can take to make reaching your goal actually happen. If you want a more accurate calculation of how much you'll need to retire on and a forecast of whether you're on track to reach it, use the Money Advice Service's pension calculator: www. moneyadviceservice.org.uk/en/tools/pension-calculator

As for how to reach that goal, start by figuring out what you already have by way of pension savings. If you've worked any full-time jobs in the past, it's very likely that you'll have a pension pot with that employer. Make a list of all your former employers and dig out your old contracts. You want to find the pension provider's name and then contact them to find out whether you have a pension pot with them and how much is in there. Also take a look at whether you're on track to receive your state pension in full. As I mentioned earlier in this chapter, you need at least 35 years of qualifying national insurance contributions. You can check your National Insurance contributions history online at www. gov.uk/check-national-insurance-record

Next, you need to decide on a pension scheme. If you're struggling to work out which of the above options (or which combination of them) is right for you, consult a financial advisor. A regulated advisor will search the whole market to find the right product for you and also offers protection should the provider go bust. You can find a financial advisor through the Money Advice Service or the FCA's directory.

Then you need to start saving! Perceived pension wisdom says in order to work out how to save into your pension, you take the age you started your pension and halve it. Use that figure as the percentage of your pre-tax salary you need to save every year until you retire. For example, if you start your pension saving at 30, you should contribute 15% of your pre-tax salary for the rest of your working life. If saving 15% of your salary into a pension sounds daunting, don't let it put you off saving altogether! It's really common for people to delay saving until they're earning more and feel like they can 'afford' it. But I want to show you that even if you're a modest saver, it's the fact you started sooner that will make the biggest difference. Say, for example, you have two savers, Sarah who starts saving for retirement at 20 by investing £50 a month into a pension pot and Joe who invests £100 a month but starts at 40. Assuming both have the same interest rate of 5%, by the time they're both 60, thanks to the effects of compound interest, Sarah's pot will be worth nearly £75,000 and Joe's only £40,000.

What distinguishes pensions from other types of savings is the boost they get from government tax relief. This is money the government would ordinarily tax you on, which instead they effectively give back to you in the form of a pension top-up. This is at the highest rate of income tax that you pay, up to £40,000 a year. Without giving yourself a headache over the maths, what you need to know is that for every £100 you pay into your pension as a basic-rate tax payer, the government adds another £25, making the total contribution £125. And if you're a higher rate payer, it's roughly £166.

So, going back to Sarah and Joe, let's say Sarah is a basic-rate tax payer. She pays her £50 a month into her pot but after her tax relief is applied, £62.50 gets paid in. Joe, meanwhile, pays tax at the 40% rate, so his £100 becomes £166. So, when you take tax relief and compound interest into account, Sarah's pot will be worth £93,000 and Joe's will be £67,600. Even though Joe contributes more each month than Sarah *and* gets more tax relief than she does, his pot is still smaller simply because she started hers sooner.

By far the best possible thing you can do for your retirement savings is to start now. Even if that means starting small. If you can't manage 15% (or whatever your ideal percentage is), any regular, manageable amount will do. They say money doesn't grow on trees, but money does grow in a pension pot if you give it enough time.

How to save for a pension when you have irregular income

If you work for an employer and contribute to a pension scheme, a nominated amount of money comes straight out of your pay cheque without you even noticing it. When you work for yourself, you have to physically transfer that money. But how can you save regularly when your income is irregular? With my savings hack! This works with any type of savings goal but I'll explain it here in relation to pensions. It's based on personal finance guru Dave Ramsey's 'hill-and-valley fund'.

A hill-and-valley fund is a savings account that helps you smooth out the ups and downs of your income. The idea is that you save money when you're at the top of the hill so that you have funds on hand to get you out of the valley. A hill-and-valley fund is *not* an emergency fund; it's more like a parking account, a place to save money for quieter months when you need a little extra to hit your savings goals.

In order to use this method, you need a dedicated bank account which will act as your hill-and-valley fund. Then you need to set up a direct debit from that account to your pension scheme. A simple way of determining how much to transfer is by asking yourself, 'How much can I afford to transfer in a month when my income is low?' By budgeting for your lowest monthly income, you'll ensure your major costs are covered first. It doesn't matter if this amount is small; it's more important that it's *regular*. You can top up your pot at any point. Once this is all set up, it's time to regularly feed your hill-and-valley account. Do this using percentages rather than fixed amounts, as this will allow for continuous saving, regardless of income fluctuations. Every time you get paid, send a percentage of your pay cheque to your hill-and-valley fund. If you're using the tax-saving technique I outlined in chapter three, you'll already be sending money to different accounts each time you get paid so just tack this habit onto that existing one.

While it's a bit of an admin headache to open another bank account, it pays off in the long run. As you get used to managing your money in this way, you can start using this account to feed other savings accounts as well. You can also simplify this process further if you switch to a digital bank like Monzo, which allows you to set up a 'pot' attached to your regular account to save for specific goals (like pensions) and from which you can pay direct debits. (NB: Any easy-access account will do here but remember that if you're making pension contributions from your limited company, the account this money is paid from has to be a business one.)

You might be thinking: this sounds like a lot of hassle, can't I just transfer into my pension when I have some spare change? Of course you can but very few of us have money left over at the end of the month and when we do, sending it to our pension pots doesn't seem appealing. By getting into the habit of paying yourself first, you make investing in your future your top priority.

Mortgages

Getting a mortgage is challenging for anyone but lenders scrutinise self-employed people even harder. By this point, it will come as no surprise that just like parental leave and pensions, mortgages for the self-employed aren't easy to secure but neither are they impossible.

Lenders primarily want to see evidence of income. Typically, they'll ask for three years of business accounts, ideally signed off by a chartered or certified accountant. They'll take an average of that income. A small handful of lenders will accept one year of accounts; however, your choice of mortgages may be limited.

If you're a sole trader, mortgage lenders will assess your profits, not your turnover. This means they look at how much you make *after* you deducted all your business expenses. So, if you make an average of £100,000 a year in sales but your profits are £60,000, the lender will give you a mortgage based on the £60,000 figure. As you'll know from chapter three, there are lots of business expenses you can deduct but while this means a smaller tax bill, be aware that if you're looking to take out a mortgage it will also mean the amount you can borrow is lower.

As a limited company director, you'll also be assessed on profits from your salary and any dividends you draw. Most lenders are only interested in money *withdrawn* from your business. So if you have £100,000 in profits in your business but only took out £20,000 in salary and dividends, then the assessment will only be based on that £20,000.

How to increase your chance of being accepted for a mortgage:

Pick the right time

How long you've been self-employed for will have an impact on your chances of getting a mortgage. Given that most lenders want to see two, or even three, years' worth of accounts, you're unlikely to get a mortgage if you've only just started freelancing. You'll also want to take your business's finances into account – has your business done well over the last three years? Have profits gone up? Are you in a good place to take on the responsibility of home ownership?

Find a broker

A mortgage broker will be able to help you navigate the challenges of self-employed mortgages. They also have access to specialist lenders who deal specifically with self-employed people. As mentioned above, different lenders have different criteria, so a good broker will be able to find you a mortgage provider that will suit your circumstances. Brokers also offer a degree of support as they'll be able to explain how the mortgage process works and advise you on your options.

Apply with someone in employment

If you're buying a property with someone who has a staff job, you might want to consider only using their income in your application. Even if you have a partner in employment, this option still might not be right for you (as I said earlier, it didn't feel right for me), however, I mention it because the reality is that mortgage applications run a lot smoother when made solely by an employee.

Hire an accountant

Mortgage lenders prefer to see accounts that were completed by an accountant rather than filed by the freelancer themselves. If you're set on buying a house in the next few years, hire an accountant to file your taxes for you.

Make sure you're on the electoral register

Regardless of whether you're a freelancer or not, making sure you're on the electoral register is a simple but important step for prospective homeowners. Lenders use data from the electoral register in their identity checks, so if you want to secure a mortgage you have to register to vote.

Fix your credit score

There's a myth that if you check your credit score, it goes down. This is true of hard credit score checks, the type that the mortgage lender will do when they run your application. But checking your score using a consumer-facing service, like Equifax or ClearScore, will not negatively impact your score.

In fact, you'll want to check your credit score before embarking on your mortgage journey in order to correct any mistakes.

Watch your loan-to-value ratio

A piece of mortgage jargon you need to know is the loan-to-value ratio. This is the amount you're borrowing in relation to the value of the house. The lower that ratio (i.e. the bigger your deposit is), the more attractive you'll look to lenders. Some lenders will accept a 10% deposit while others will want to see up to 25%. In any case, the bigger your deposit, the lower the interest rate will be on your repayment.

What you need to know about mortgage repayments and tax-deductible expenses

As you'll remember from chapter three, there are plenty of tax-deductible business expenses you can claim. When you own your home, the rules about what you can expense when you work from home are slightly different than for renters.

If you're a sole trader, you can only claim your mortgage *interest* – not the repayments of the capital. Remember, you can only claim some of that interest as it pertains to the proportion of the house you use as a working space.

As a limited company, you have the option to 'rent' your home office to your business. In effect, you draw up a rental agreement between you and your limited company, charging yourself rent that you can then claim as an expense. Whether or not this option is right for you depends on a number of factors so it's important to seek advice from your accountant before doing it.

Chapter Summary: Freelancing and Families

Adulting as a freelancer isn't easy but by planning ahead and understanding what rights you have and what benefits you can claim, you can make it work.

Parental leave and pay: While birth mothers may be able to claim Maternity Allowance, self-employed fathers and partners have no equivalent.

Pensions: Freelancers are entitled to a state pension but it's not enough to cover their retirement so it's vital to open a private pension plan as soon as possible.

Mortgages: It is possible to buy a house as a self-employed person, just be prepared for extra admin and longer waiting times.

FREELANCER STORY

Emilie Bellet (@vestpod) – founder of Vestpod

I'd worked in banking and finance for eight years. I wanted to leave for a long time but when you've done a corporate job for so long, it's hard to know what you're capable of doing. I thought I had very niche skills that weren't transferable but that just wasn't true.

When I did eventually leave, I set up a tech startup so I wasn't really on my own because I was working for investors. It was a good way for me to leave the corporate finance world but, at the same time, I didn't feel like I had full freedom and flexibility and I realised the mission I was working on wasn't the right one for me. That startup actually ended up failing. Leaving the corporate world to

---

start with a failure was pretty tough but I learned so much from the experience. It gave me the courage to keep going until I found my mission and what I really wanted to work on.

After that, I set up Vestpod, a digital platform that aims to change the conversation about money and empower women financially. I started it from home, using my savings to build the website, and I started producing content to build up the community. It's been a huge jump from the corporate world to freelancing, to say the least. All three of my kids were born while I was working on my business. I can't pretend it was easy but I love it. I have to be really focused on my priorities to make it all work but I wouldn't have it any other way. Because I work from home, I get to spend a lot of time with my kids. I wouldn't have been able to spend anywhere near as much time as I do with my children had I stayed in the finance industry. I left early in the morning and came home late at night. It was a demanding job and I was always on call, constantly checking my email. Now, because I manage my own time, I know that I can go half a day without checking my inbox and everything is fine. I can't imagine going to an office job now. It's a huge privilege to be able to see my children as much as I do.

When I left finance to do something else, it was really hard. I left a high-paying job with good prospects. When I left, people told me I was crazy. But what I didn't realise is that when you leave the corporate world, there are so many opportunities. You just have to find them and embrace change. This is something you're not taught to do in the corporate world. But for me, I found out just how creative I really am and I'm really grateful to have learned that and to get to work in this way.

Part Three:

Future-proof Your Freelancing

CHAPTER ELEVEN

When Things Go Wrong

In my first year of freelancing, I lost a major client and I got super sick.

First, it was the client. Within the first couple of months of self-employment, I had freelancing's holy grail in my hands – a regular client. It was a big deal for me to land them and, for the best part of a year, they provided the backbone of my income. I lost them because the company ended up hiring a full-time staffer whose job it became to do the work I was doing. I'd had it easy with freelancing up until that point as that gig was bringing in reliable income.

Not long after that, I got sick. A mystery illness landed me in hospital for a couple of nights. It took me nearly a month to recover and because the problem was in my eye, spending eight hours a day at the computer was out of the question. Not only was I unwell but I was also freaking out about work. At that point, because of what had happened with the client, I was juggling lots of new assignments and I didn't know when I'd be back on my feet. It was one of the rare points in my freelancing journey that I wished I was working in a staff job. All I wanted was to be signed off from work, still get my pay cheque and not have to worry. After this experience, I put measures in place should things go south for me again – a few small changes that would protect me in the worse-case scenario. I'm so glad I did because during the 2020 pandemic I relied heavily on these protocols.

Of course, things can and do go wrong when you work for an employer but when you're self-employed you feel more alone in dealing with these issues. To start with, you don't have the cushion of sick pay, compassionate leave or holiday days that most employers offer. Something bad happening can be very isolating, especially when the mistake is something you feel responsible for, like messing up your taxes or losing a client. At the same time, the absence of an HR department doesn't mean the situation is hopeless.

So consider this the 'break glass in case of emergency' chapter. It's a freelancer's recovery kit containing everything you need to get you through a crisis, as well as the tools to help prevent it from happening in the first place.

In this chapter, you'll learn:

- How to tackle the most common problems freelancers face
- Tips for protecting yourself and your work
- An action plan for if things go really wrong

First Aid for Freelancers

Problem #1: The freelance work dries up

Here's what to do if you're experiencing the dreaded freelance lull.

Assess the situation

There's a huge difference between having a quiet period and being in a dire financial position. More often than not, the situation isn't as bad as you imagine it to be. In fact, a quiet couple of weeks in the grand scheme of an otherwise profitable freelance business is really nothing to stress about. If you've been freelancing long enough, compare this period to the same time last year – is this just a quiet time of year for you (and your industry) in general?

You also need to take a deep breath and look at your bank account. Often when freelancers are quiet, they also assume they're broke but that isn't necessarily the case. Remember to also look at your outstanding invoices to see what's coming in and when. Taking that first step, as awful as it might feel, will give you the information you need to figure out what to do next.

It's so easy to forget this in the midst of a lull but it's very normal for freelance work to go up and down. When I first started out, it happened a lot more because I hadn't figured out a good pitching rhythm yet so would find myself completing an assignment and then not having something else to work on. The work hadn't actually dried up, I just didn't have the hang of riding the freelancing wave just yet.

Pitch, pitch, pitch

The cold hard truth of it is that the only way out of a lack of work is to pitch for more of it. I say that in the full knowledge that when you feel downtrodden or low in confidence, putting yourself out there feels unbearable. The sales and marketing tools in chapters six and seven will help immensely should you find yourself in this situation.

As a refresher, start by reaching out to clients you've worked with before and those in your immediate network. If they don't have any work, ask them for an introduction to colleagues in other departments who might need your services. It's also a good idea to ask previous clients for a referral that you can use on your website or social media. As well as being a helpful marketing tool, it will also give you a much needed confidence boost to hear how good you are at your job.

When you're going through a dry spell, it's important to be aware of how you're pitching yourself so that you don't slip into a scarcity mindset. There is enough work to go around; don't shoot yourself in the foot by sending panicked, incomprehensible emails to random people. If you're pitching for new work, pick your best ideas, flesh them out into compelling email queries and send them to the places that would be an actual fit.

If you're posting on social media that you're looking for work, frame it positively. For example, rather than posting on LinkedIn or Twitter that you have no work and can't pay your bills, write something like: *I've got space in my schedule to take on some new clients in the coming weeks. As a reminder, I'm a digital copywriter specialising in food writing and here's how you can contact me.*

Plan rather than panic

If you're in a position where a quiet week won't damage your overall financial health then use it to think about planning for the future. It may be unexpected downtime but there's another way to look at this situation: as an opportunity to plan for it to not happen again.

Here are some actions you can take:

- Take an afternoon to do a review of your situation. What are the opportunities you're missing? Do you need to reassess how you schedule your week in order to incorporate more time for developing and sending pitches? Does your website need updating? What marketing worked for you in the past and can you do more of it? What about your outgoings? Are there subscriptions you can cancel or could you switch to a cheaper mobile phone or insurance provider?
- Think about upskilling. If you've noticed that there's a particular skill that clients keep asking you for that you don't have, consider investing in training to learn it.
- Apply for part-time jobs so that you introduce some regular income into your cash flow. Search on jobs boards for part-time opportunities and send in a few applications.
- Join an agency, freelance collective or online marketplace. After you pass the application stage, these platforms will find work on your behalf, usually for a small percentage of your fee. (I've listed some in the directory at the end of this book.)
- Team up with other freelancers to offer complementary skills. For example, if you're a copywriter you could pair up with a web designer to offer a package by posting on social media or in an online freelance group, or make use of their network.

Whatever it is, just make the best possible use of this time. If you've spent a morning firing off pitches, accept that clients aren't going to reply to you immediately and do something else. Do your files need backing up? Are there other projects you can work on? You definitely have expenses that need filing.

Look after yourself

This always applies but don't neglect your mental and physical health during a dry patch. Don't chain yourself to your desk. Eat, sleep and exercise properly. If working from home alone is making the situation worse, ask a freelance friend to co-work with you. Talk to people; ask for help.

Problem #2: You lose a major client

Regular work with a reliable client is the holy grail of freelancing, and if you lose that, it's pretty devastating. Here's what to do if you lose a major client:

Take a beat

Just like being made redundant, losing a big client is a shock. You may need some time to adjust to what's happened, especially if it came as a surprise. There's no shame in needing a moment's pause when something unexpected happens in your career.

While a period of grieving can be helpful, it's important not to dwell on what happened or to internalise the rejection. It's very easy when something like this sets us back to take it personally and to internalise it as a failing on our part. Do whatever it takes to build that confidence back up by taking good care of your mental wellbeing. Revisit the strategies for this in chapter eight.

This is also a good moment to run your numbers. It's important to know how big that financial hole is that you now need to plug. Go over your accounts and see how much you were bringing in each month from that company. Do this straight away. Don't bury your head in the sand about it.

Be real about what actually happened

Once you're feeling up to it, it's worth asking yourself the tough questions about what went wrong. It might be the case that the contract came to its natural end. In which case, perhaps the lesson is to plan so that next time, you look for new work sooner so there's less of a gap between projects.

If the loss of the contract was more unexpected, however, or if the client terminated the project, then it's important to figure out why. The best way to do that is to simply ask them for clear and constructive feedback so you can improve in the future. It's always better to know why something happened than to fill in the blanks yourself.

Use it as an opportunity

There are two ways of looking at what's happened when you lose a big client. One is dwelling on the raw figure of the financial hit you're taking each month. The other is appreciating all the time you've just got back to either launch that project you've been meaning to for ages or land a new, better paid gig.

In every downturn lies an opportunity to rebuild. Often a setback can be the kick up the bum we need to take a leap of faith. Do you have a dream project you've been putting off because of a lack of time? Now would be a great moment to use that newly freed-up time to figure out a way to make it a reality.

Problem #3: A client refuses to pay you

An all-too common problem freelancers face is late payments. In chapter one, I explained how to deal with late paying clients, but here's what to do if they outright refuse to pay you.

Figure out if it's worth taking action

If a client refuses to pay you, you first have to figure out if it's worth taking action against them. Pursuing a claim can be costly and time consuming and, depending on whether you had a contract, may be hard to prove. It's also important to factor in whether the company will pay even if you win – if they've gone bankrupt, you probably won't be able to recoup the money. It's worth seeking legal advice to get an opinion on the strength of your claim before deciding what to do next – in many cases, a letter from a lawyer will be all that's needed to resolve the matter. If you can't afford a lawyer, the Citizens Advice Bureau may be able to help. (See page 15 for more information about late payments.)

Turn to your union or professional association

If you're a member of a union or a trade association like the Association for Independent Professionals and the Self-Employed (IPSE), they can help. For a freelancer, union membership acts as an insurance policy against things going wrong, so it's advisable to call your representative in these situations. They will have access to legal advice and will be able to help you decide your next steps. If you do decide to take legal action, they can also do this on your behalf.

Use a mediation service

You can attempt to resolve the issue without taking legal action by using a mediation service. The Civil Mediation Council has a directory of approved mediators who can help you. This will involve a fee. It's less aggressive than taking legal action but still a formalised process.

Take them to the small claims court

The small claims court handles cases for amounts of up to £10,000. The system is designed to make it easy to make a claim (you can do it online) and you don't need a lawyer. You will have to pay a fee but if you win you may be able to claim it back. The fees vary from £25 to £410, depending on the size of the claim. When you make a claim, you will have to gather evidence to submit to the court and you'll also have to attend court dates.

Problem #5: You mess up your tax return

In the first 18 months of freelancing, you need to get your head around a lot of things. Chief among them is filing your own tax return. The first self-assessment is always the hardest and if you aren't prepared for it, you can easily find yourself in a situation in which you can't cover your tax bill.

If you make a mistake with your taxes, first of all, know that you're not alone. Roughly one in five people think they've submitted their forms with an error on them, according to HMRC. If you do make a mistake, or if you can't pay your tax bill by the deadline, you need to call HMRC.

If you contact the tax authority, they will be able to work with you to rectify the situation. According to HMRC, if you contact them as soon as you can, you may be able to get more time to pay or they may work out a repayment instalment plan for you. By taking early action, you'll not only have a greater chance of HMRC being lenient with you, it will also put your mind at ease sooner.

When you call them, just explain to them what happened. We're all scared of the 'tax man' but in reality, it's a person at the other end of the phone. Being honest is your best option because you do intend to fix the problem. You're not trying to evade the system; you just made a mistake.

Problem #6: You get sick

If you get sick as a freelancer, the most important thing is to put your health first. Even if you just have a cold, don't be tempted to work through it just because you don't have an office to call in sick to. If you take time off to recover fully, you'll get better faster.

Let your clients know what's going on. Everyone gets sick and there's nothing you can do about it. Your clients *will* understand that, especially if you let them know as soon as possible so that they can make alternative arrangements if needed. It's also fine if you don't know when you'll be able to go back to work – just keep your client updated. You don't have to go into details about the nature of your illness if you don't feel comfortable doing so but do let them know you can't work for medical reasons.

If your illness goes on for more than a week or if you do end up losing work because of it, now is the time to use any emergency savings you have (or your benefits package – more on that later). Many of us are good at saving but not so great at actually using the money. That money will buy you peace of mind to rest until you're back on your feet. That's why you saved it up in the first place. Plus, replenishing those savings will be a lot easier when you're in good health.

When you feel better, ease back into work. Spend the first day back at your desk auditing all your work and making a plan for how you'll tackle it. You will probably find that, though you had different deadlines for all your projects before you got sick, now everything has stacked up against each other. You're not going to be able to get it all done at the same time so prioritise and let your clients know a revised – and realistic – deadline.

Getting sick can also give some much needed perspective about work and life. Health is so important – mental as much as physical. When you build a freelance career doing what you love, it's inevitable that work becomes part of your identity. But there has to be more to your life than work.

Protecting Yourself

Know your risks and rights

Freelancing is risky business in some ways, but you do also have plenty of rights. It's important to know the difference between the real risks and those you can be protected against. For example, you do have a right to get paid on time. You don't, however, have any rights to claim sick pay.

Too often companies hide behind a false narrative that there's nothing a freelancer can do if they come up against bad behaviour. That's not true! There are plenty of steps you can take to protect yourself as a freelancer so that if something unexpected happens it feels like a bump in the road rather than something that completely derails you.

Contracts

If anything client-related goes wrong, the first question that a lawyer will ask is whether you had a contract. Many clients don't provide their freelancers with contracts as standard but you should always ask for one regardless. If the client doesn't want to provide one (many don't and are under no obligation to do so for freelancers), you can prepare one yourself. As full contracts are complicated to write, your best option is to have one drawn up by a legal expert. It's not as involved or expensive as you might think. I've paid £300 for a template contract which I've used for multiple clients. Given what can go wrong if you don't have a contract, it's more than worth the investment.

You can access contract templates through a professional body or union or you can buy them from a legal service. Some freelancer platforms, such as Underpinned (www.under-pinned.co) and the Freelancer Club (www.freelancerclub.net), offer a contract template designed specifically for freelancers.

If you'd rather DIY it, you can also ask for what's known as a statement of work, letter of engagement or work agreement. These are like 'light' contracts which basically set out in plain English the basic terms of the project, like the project fee, the description of the services you will provide and the deadlines. You can write this up yourself and both parties can sign it.

What if the client won't sign anything?

You can't legally force a client to sign a contract or a work agreement. If you're coming up against this situation, it's important to assess why they don't want to sign. Sometimes, smaller clients don't want the hassle of drawing up contracts. If a client is reticent to commit anything in writing, start by explaining to them that it's in their interest as well as yours.

If you really can't get a client to sign anything, think carefully about whether you really want to do business with them. If you do, at the very least make sure there is an email containing all the critical details about the project.

Emergency fund

The best way to protect yourself against things going wrong is by having an emergency fund. You might already have one of these for your personal finances – it's really up to you whether you want to have a completely separate 'freelance emergency fund' as well. Either way, this money is for unpredictable situations outside of day-to-day spending. Things that, if they happened and you didn't deal with them, would knock your life and/or career off course. A.K.A. emergencies! These include your laptop breaking, a client suing you, an unexpected insurance bill, your car breaking down, a living situation emergency. The point of the emergency fund is so you don't have to rely on someone else to bail you out or max out a credit card that will get you into debt.

The amount you need will vary but a good starting goal to aim for is £1,000. If you don't have a spare grand lying around, think about saving a little bit every day. If you put £3.50 into a savings account every day for 10 months you will have £1,000. If you put £5 aside a day, you'll get there in seven months. To help top up your savings, take advantage of the mobile banks and apps that will round up your spare change. That £2.95 take-away coffee gets rounded up to £3 and 5p goes into a savings or investment account for you. So you quite literally save without having to think about it.

Wherever you save this money, just make sure it's completely separate from your daily spending account and that it's easy to access.

Provide your own benefits package

One big downside of freelancing is the lack of benefits and perks you get as a company employee. When you work for yourself, it's really important to take into account that you don't get things like holiday, sick or maternity pay. If you think about it, though, being freelance means being the boss and the employee at the same time. So it's on you to provide yourself with good perks. Rather than seeing a lack of corporate perks as just the way things are, why not build yourself a benefits package worthy of a corporate job? When you're self-employed, good benefits are less about bullshit corporate perks and more about giving yourself some breathing room. Whereas an emergency fund is for paying for unexpected expenses, a benefits package gives you income when you don't have it. You'll need to rely on your benefits package any time you want to take time off, whether that's for a holiday or if you get sick. Or if you're planning on taking parental leave at some point, this money will enable you to take an extended period of time off. You can also use this pot of money as a buffer for situations in which a client is overdue on a payment.

In order to build up this fund, first, set aside one month's worth of your *essential* living expenses (rent, groceries and utilities) and work towards building that up to three months' worth. Again, use percentages to top up these savings – every time you get paid, send a percentage of that income to your benefits package savings account. Like the emergency fund, you want to keep this money fairly liquid but separate from your regular spending.

Insurance

Depending on your personal circumstances and the type of freelancing you do, you may want to take out insurance. There are different types of insurance available for freelancers, which I've listed here.

TYPES OF INSURANCE

Professional liability: This type of insurance protects you against claims that your work was faulty. For example, if you are a graphic designer and get sued for copyright infringement for a logo you designed that looks similar to another company's design.

General liability: This covers property damage or injury caused by you or that happens on your premises. For example, if you're a freelance hairdresser who works from home and a client trips over the hairdryer cable and injures themselves and sues you.

Equipment insurance: This cover insures your gear in case something happens to it. If you work from home, it's important to check if your home insurance covers your equipment, because many policies need you to declare if you also use it for work.

Income protection: This protects you if your earnings drop because of sickness and injury.

Critical illness cover: This is a long-term insurance policy which pays out a tax-free lump sum if you are diagnosed with a serious illness.

Whether or not you need insurance comes down to your specific circumstances and what work you do. For example, freelancers who regularly have clients visit their home office are more likely to need general liability cover. Or if you're a photographer with a lot of expensive gear, you may need equipment cover.

If you're thinking about getting insurance, do your research first and make sure you fully understand what the policy offers. Shop around and compare policies – banks and building societies, as well as online insurers and comparison sites, are all good places to look. The government's Money Advice Service recommends talking to a special insurance broker if you're considering a complex policy like income protection or critical illness cover. You can find a broker through the British Insurance Brokers Association (www.insurance.biba.org.uk).

Unions and industry bodies

As a freelancer, you have two main options for joining a professional body – you can either join a trade union or a professional association. In industries in which freelancing is common, like journalism, entertainment and acting, the freelancing branch of the union tends to be strong.

The main advantage of joining a union is legal assistance. As a freelancer, you aren't joining a union to ensure you get better treatment in the workplace; you're protecting yourself in case something goes wrong. Your union membership should include access to free legal advice and in cases of a dispute, the union will take court action on your behalf. Unions also offer their members training and professional development courses, as well as advice for best practice.

Unions tend to have a reputation for taking the worker's side and taking a hard line against employer malpractice. This isn't necessarily a bad thing but it's worth considering what kind of reputation your union has within the industry.

The alternative to a union is a professional association or cooperative. This can be a smaller, industry-specific association, a grassroots collective or a sector-wide self-employed body. The Association of Independent Professionals and the Self-Employed is the UK's largest freelancers' association.

Association membership benefits are similar to those of a union but the focus is usually more on professional development and business skills. As such, resources tend to be more up to date with the goings on in the industry. Professional associations do also offer legal assistance as well as tax help and some provide insurance too.

If you're considering a union membership or joining a professional association, start by asking yourself what's important to you. Do you need tax or legal help? Is it template contracts you're after? Or do you need training? Will you make use of the membership? Are you paying for peace of mind? Don't forget that you can expense the cost of either a union or association membership on your tax return. The price of a membership will vary depending on your industry but typically will cost a couple of hundred pounds a year.

Freelancer's resilience

There are lots of things you can buy to protect yourself as a freelancer but perhaps the best investment you can make is in your resilience. If our mental and emotional reserves are low, tackling the curve balls that freelance life throws at us can be draining.

You'll remember from chapter eight that resilience is a practice that's found in the daily steps we take to look after our mental and physical health. Getting enough sleep, eating well, doing exercise, having a strong support network, being part of a freelance community, practising gratitude and mindfulness are all part of a strong freelance armour. Resilience building is something that we have to do when things are going well so that if they go badly, we have the reserves to bounce back.

The Freelancer's Crisis Action Plan

Sometimes, things can go really wrong in our freelancing. If you're facing a major disaster that's threatening your business, like a recession, use my crisis action plan to weather the storm.

Step one: Put your oxygen mask on

Before you can take care of your business, first you have to take care of yourself. This checklist will help you make sure your health and wellbeing are in the best place they can be.

Wellbeing checklist

How am I taking care of myself? Am I getting enough sleep, eating properly and moving my body?

Am I communicating with others about how I'm feeling? Tell those you're sharing your space with how you're doing, especially if you're struggling.

Am I relaxing? You might be at home with not much to do but that doesn't necessarily mean you're able to relax properly. Prioritising rest right now is more important than ever.

Am I breathing properly? This might sound ridiculous but how we breathe affects our stress levels. When we're anxious, shallow breathing makes our anxiety worse.

How is what I'm letting into my orbit affecting me? Consider limiting your news and social media consumption and setting boundaries around what you let pop up on your phone.

Do I know my own warning signs? Each of us responds differently in times of crisis – are you feeling angry or irritable or crying more than usual? Are you tuning into what your body is telling you it needs?

Am I being compassionate? Be kind to yourself and others right now. There is no 'wrong' way to feel.

Step two: Draw the purse strings

Second to the threat of the crisis itself is the economic impact it will leave in its wake. Many freelancers will have periods where they lose work and will worry about where the next pay cheque will come from. It's time to draw the purse strings.

Financial health checklist

Audit your finances: Assess your personal situation as soon as you can. If you have money in savings or an emergency fund, now is the time to use it. If you are a member of a union or a professional body, find out if they're able to support you. If you are struggling to pay bills, talk to your creditors straight away.

Chase invoices: Allow no invoice to go unpaid. Also, make sure you are sending invoices for ongoing work as promptly as possible. If you have an overdue invoice, email your client about it. Remember to be polite and to the point. Ask for a date when you can expect to be paid and if there's a contact in the accounts department who you can speak to directly.

Cut expenditure: Go through your outgoings and cut back on anything non-essential. A good rule of thumb is to ask yourself, 'Will this cost help my business in some way right now?' If yes, keep it. If no, either freeze it or cancel it.

Step three: Recalibrate

Many crises, like recessions or pandemics, are not short term. If it looks like you're in it for the long haul, start making small steps to adapt to your new normal.

The recalibration checklist

Accept that productivity looks very different right now: While you might already be used to working from home, you're probably struggling to concentrate in a time of crisis. Lower your expectations and be kind to yourself. If you're used to working 9am to 5pm, aim for 9am till 1pm instead. If you're balancing looking after kids with work, know that doing your best is more than good enough. If all you achieve today is getting through another day, recognise how truly important that is.

Change your routine if it's not working for you: Routines, rituals and structure can bring some semblance of normality in chaotic times. However, the routine you used to rely on may no longer work for you. You also may need a different routine every day, depending on how you're feeling. Be flexible and find a routine that's baggy enough to give you room to breathe.

Communicate with clients: Stay in contact with your current clients. If you have an ongoing project, ask them if the deadlines or expectations have changed. Try to get a sense of what is happening on your client's end – is their business in trouble and how might this affect you? If you're struggling to meet deadlines, let them know as soon as possible. Also, let your clients know if you're available to help them right now. Tell them if you're willing to take on additional work or expand your services or if you're available for fast turn-around projects.

Step four: Work on your business rather than in it

Even in times when your work is on hold, it's never gone completely. A crisis is only ever temporary and once it passes, work will resume. In the meantime, there's plenty to get on with if you need a distraction.

Work checklist

Define your why: Do you have a guiding principle that informs your freelance business? A purpose, something that drives you to do what you do. Your why. A classic example is Apple – their why is 'to think differently'. This is a big exercise to do but one that will pay dividends down the road. To figure out your why, start by thinking about what lights you up, what your strengths are and where you add value. For a refresher on finding your why, refer back to chapter six on DIY Marketing.

Do your admin: If you want to tackle an equally important but less thinky task, do your admin. Fix your website; tidy up your LinkedIn profile; re-write your Twitter bio; archive your work. If you can face it, file your expenses.

Spring clean your work: Have you been promising yourself that you'll find a new piece of bookkeeping software or will look into project management tools? Or maybe your digital files are in a mess? Now is the time to fix the things that aren't working for you. Think of this as the business equivalent of organising your cupboards.

Chapter Summary: When Things Go Wrong

Things can and do go wrong when you work for yourself. No matter what challenges are thrown your way, know that you can deal with them using the following strategies.

Pause: If something goes wrong, the first thing to do is take a moment to catch your breath. Make sure to look after your wellbeing in a time of crisis.

Plan before you panic: In our worst moments, it's easy to feel like our problems are too big for us to handle. Take a step back to figure out what is within your control to change versus what you're catastrophising. Ask yourself: what action can I take to improve this situation?

Ask for help: Depending on what's gone wrong, there are various places you can turn to for help, including legal services.

Protect yourself: Once you've passed through the storm, it's time to prepare should something happen again. Trade unions, professional associations and insurance policies can all help protect you and your business in the future.

CHAPTER TWELVE

In It for the Long Haul

Should you just get a real job?

Yes, you read that question correctly. You're now 12 chapters into a book about working for yourself and I just asked if maybe you should stop working for yourself. In order to explain myself, first I need to talk about quitting.

I still remember the day I handed in my resignation letter to my boss and quit my first grown-up job. I didn't sleep the night before and I spent all morning nervously sat at my desk, trying to work out when would be the right time for me to print out my letter and ask my boss for a moment of her time. I kept looking at the clock and promising myself that when the time hit a round number – 20 minutes past, 30 minutes past, ten to the hour – I'd ask her for a chat. When I finally squeaked out my request for five minutes of her time, my ears rang as we walked over to the meeting room.

Quitting is not something that any of us like doing. We're actively told that quitting is a Bad Thing. In a world in which growth, drive and ambition are fetishised, quitting is synonymous with giving up. But sometimes we just have to let go. I did manage to hand in that letter of resignation and I left that job to do a master's degree in journalism. That year changed the course of my career and indeed my life; had I not been brave enough to admit to myself that job was no longer working for me, I wouldn't be where I am now.

I say all this because a life-long career as a freelancer isn't for everyone. That's fine. Working for yourself doesn't have to be forever. It can be something you dip in and out of over the course of a long career. It can be a stepping stone to a full-time staff job. It can be a breather while you work things out. You might want to quit the way you work, who you work for, or even your specialism in search of something different. You might also find that you want to continue working for yourself but in a different capacity. Working for yourself can be whatever you want it to be because it's your job, your career, your life.

When I started working for myself, I had no idea if I wanted to do it forever. I'm fairly certain now that I do but it's not a decision I've carved into stone. Despite what college career advisors would have you think, there's no such thing as forever when it comes to your work. And if you do decide that you're in the self-employment game for the long haul, that throws up new and different kinds of uncertainties. How will I sustain this for years to come? How can I ensure that I'm still developing in my career when I don't have a corporate structure around me?

In this chapter, I'll dive into the core principles of taking a business of one to its next stages but first I'm going to help you figure out what you really want from your career.

In this chapter, you'll learn:

- It's OK to quit
- How to promote yourself when you don't have a boss

- How to streamline your business and maximise efficiency
- The six basics of growing a business

How to Know When to Quit

In 2018, the leadership coach and creative entrepreneur Sarah Weiler gave a TED talk in which she posited the idea that quitting should be championed. She said: 'This isn't about quitting being better than staying. This is about asking a different question altogether. *Does it still serve me to be here?*'

Since delivering the talk, Weiler went on to create her Quitting Quadrant (www.quittingquadrant.com), a framework for working out whether it's time to let something go and move on. She found that often people wait until they reach breaking point to decide whether it's time to stop doing something because of the shame and guilt associated with quitting.

Sometimes, we end up quitting something because we don't know how to distinguish between feeling disinterest or just discomfort. The former is a sign we should move on, while the latter just means the work is hard. Weiler wanted to create a tool that allowed people to regularly check in with their projects, jobs and responsibilities so they could be more aware of what they actually need and avoid unnecessary downward spirals.

The basic idea of the quadrant is that there are four healthy states we're in when working on something: flow (hyper focus, the things that feel rewarding), grit (things we need to get through to get things done), restore (taking a break) and growth (new projects, where we're developing skills). We need to be moving through all four states to feel happy and fulfilled in our work. But when we spend too long in one state, we go into a negative expression. Flow becomes plateau, grit becomes resentment, growth becomes burnout and restore becomes apathy. It's in those negative expressions that quitting happens.

'I call it the Quitting Quadrant because it brings awareness to the very fine line between loving your work and completely overwhelming yourself,' Weiler explained. The framework helps you take your temperature on any given project in order to help you work out whether to continue it or to let it go. Rather than wait until you're burned out or resentful, you assess a situation before the crisis hits.

I used the Quitting Quadrant when I was trying to figure out whether to stop working with a particular client. I was perpetually frustrated by them but kept telling myself the money was good and I felt stuck in a vicious cycle. I turned to the quadrant to help me untangle my feelings and work out what to do next. Weiler's exercises got me to ask myself whether the project was high or low interest to me and then whether it was high or low discomfort. After answering those questions, I found myself firmly in the resentment quadrant. I wasn't engaged with the work; it wasn't stimulating me and caused me a great deal of stress. I did quit that project in the end and it was thanks to the quadrant that I was able to see why that was the right decision for me at that point.

Weiler, who works for herself, told me the quadrant can be used by freelancers for projects large and small, from deciding whether to pull out of a talk to figuring out whether freelancing is still right for you. 'Most people are only in the habit of checking in when things are at breaking point,' Weiler says. 'The quadrant gives you a snapshot of your life which you can use on a regular basis to zoom out and see where everything is in that moment.'

Going Back into a Staff Role After Freelancing

As I wrote at the beginning of this chapter, there are lots of reasons why you might decide to return to an in-house position after some time working for yourself. A staff job might fit better with a change in your circumstances; you might miss being part of a team; or you just don't find joy in self-employment anymore. Whatever the reason, here are my top tips for applying for staff jobs after a period of freelancing:

Give yourself the permission to do it

It's OK to get a staff job if that's what you want to do! During the height of the pandemic, I heard from countless freelancers who wanted to find a staff job but were ashamed of their decision. They didn't want to look like they couldn't make freelancing work and felt guilty that they wanted to be told what to do by a boss.

Once you've decided you want to start looking for a staff role, the first thing to do is give yourself the permission to accept your decision. Job hunting is bad enough without also feeling like you're a failure for choosing that path.

Write your CV in their language

A common stumbling block for finding a staff job after free-lancing is accurately presenting your skills so they make sense to a potential employer. As you well know, working for yourself looks quite different from staff work and, as such, you need to translate your experience into language employers can parse.

Traditional CVs aren't designed to showcase the skills and expertise of someone who's worked for themselves. Rather than bundling all your freelance work under one heading, list your most relevant projects as individual entries as though they were discrete jobs. This will help a recruiter view your experience in a way they can understand.

Find a job that gives you the bits of freelancing you did like

If you're leaving the freelance world, chances are there are aspects of it that weren't for you. But it's likely you also did enjoy some parts of it. Get clear on what those parts were and seek out staff roles that still enable you to benefit from them. For example, you might have enjoyed working from home but hated doing your admin and finding clients. In which case, a remote job might be for you. Or perhaps you enjoyed the variety of working for different clients but found it lonely working by yourself – so look for agency roles. If freelancing was all about the flexibility, enabling you to work around your family commitments, find companies that respect working families and have progressive attitudes towards flexible working.

Prepare for the question 'Why don't you want to freelance anymore?'

If you've been working for yourself for a number of years, a recruiter is bound to ask why you want to stop doing that in order to work for someone else. It's an inappropriate question if you think about it – what's it really got to do with whether or not you can do the job? – but they love to ask it, so you need a good answer. Some answers you could give in response to this question are:

- I want to be part of a team as I do my best work in collaboration with others, working together to solve problems and supporting one another
- I want to focus on one project with a central mission, giving it all my creative energy
- I want to play a central role in shaping a company, rather than being the outsider coming in temporarily

How to Promote Yourself When You Don't Have a Boss

When you work alone, there's no one to push you around. There's also no one to *push* you. Without a boss, you don't have someone to mark your progress, someone who can encourage you to take on more responsibility, expand your role, bring on change. In other words, if you want a promotion when you work for yourself, you have to do it yourself.

There's no 'Senior Freelancer' job title, so what does a promotion even look like when you don't have a boss?

Promotions are no longer about status for me and are instead about celebrating my achievements and developing my skills. Isn't that what a promotion is when you break it down, anyway? A recognition of the work you do and a development of your role to include more responsibilities. Here are some ways to promote yourself when you don't have a boss:

CEO Days

Jen Carrington, creative coach and co-host of the podcast *Letters to a Hopeful Creative*, advocates for what she calls 'CEO days'. These are days blocked out in her diary to work on, rather than in, her business.

'Have a CEO day at least once a month, if not every two weeks or so, so you can be constantly checking in with the business and making purposeful and intentional plans of action so you know each month, week and day what needs to be done,' she writes on her blog.

The aim of CEO days is to look at the big picture stuff and make sure your business is moving forward. Carrington recommends asking the following questions:

- Do I have a clear business plan and model guiding me along the way? If not, how can I prioritise making some time to work on that?
- What are the core areas of focus and priorities for the next 6–18 months in my business? What do I need to put in place to make the day-to-day running of my business more productive and focused?
- What core goals do I want to work towards in my business in this season and how am I practically going to make them happen?

Give yourself better perks

In the previous chapter, I talked about the importance of starting a benefits package, a fund to cover things like time off, sick days and any other times you need some extra income in your business.

As you grow your business of one, start thinking about how to use your benefits package to provide you with extra perks. Maybe you want to take a working holiday in a rustic cottage, or perhaps you want to go down to a four-day week, or you might want to invest in private medical insurance or a training course. Start taking steps to give yourself the employee perks that you want.

Hire an assistant

There's more on growing your business through outsourcing later in this chapter but if you want to take on more ambitious projects, it's time to bring in someone to take care of the clerical work. Hiring a freelance assistant can free up your time in order for you to focus on new projects or getting a new business idea off the ground. It also feels very executive to have an assistant, a perk that comes with a big promotion.

Praise yourself

One way to promote yourself is to keep recognising the value of your own work. No one else will do that for you, so keep patting yourself on your back. In chapter eight, I wrote about the praise folder, a place to collect the positive feedback you get about your work to read back on the days you aren't feeling confident. If you don't have a praise folder, start one. Also get in the habit of writing down your little wins throughout the day. Start a document of little wins and at the end of the week, read them back to yourself.

Create a bonus system

There's no Christmas bonus when you work for yourself. Unless you create one. One way to do this is by putting aside more than you need for your tax bill throughout the year and using the surplus to treat yourself when it comes to paying it. That serves the double whammy of being a welcome surprise when it comes to doing your taxes and incentivising you to actually file them on time. Or you can automate your bonus – if you use a bank account or app that rounds up your spending, use the money from that at the end of each year as your 'bonus'.

Work Less, Do More: How to Grow Your Business

In traditional business speak, a well known method for growing a business is through improving its efficiency. You do this by increasing productivity and reducing overheads. While productivity is an economic measure and tracks the health of national economies and multinational corporations, it's also a personal metric in your freelance business. When you work for yourself, your personal productivity *is* the measure of the health of your business.

So how do you improve the efficiency of your freelance business? Your aim is to produce more work – and therefore generate more income – but to spend less time and energy on that production. The idea isn't to work more, quite the opposite. It's to get more done while spending the same, or even less, time doing it. There are four key areas to work on the efficiency of your business.

People

If you worked at the senior management level of a company and were tasked with improving efficiency, the first thing you'd look at is your headcount. How many people work for you and are they doing a good job? When you have a large staff, improving efficiency usually means reducing your headcount. But I'm obviously not going to tell you to fire yourself. On the contrary – perhaps it's time to hire people?

When you're the only member of staff, you drain your efficiency by doing work that you could pay someone else to do faster and better than you can. This is especially true of clerical or administrative work when your company is thriving and you're having to turn down work.

Here are the different types of support you can hire:

- Agents: literary agent, podcast, content creator, TV and film. These people work for you, they take a cut of your fees but they help you to develop your career. I have two agents; one handles my literary work (she helped me land this book deal!) and the other handles all my speaking and presenting work. Increasingly, specialist agencies focused on representing digital content creators are popping up.

- Virtual assistants: To handle your diary management, emails, scheduling, and other admin.
- Bookkeepers and accountants: To do your tax returns but also to keep an eye on your cashflow and to help you make better-informed business decisions.
- Other freelancers: To help you execute your projects.

Systems and processes

Over the last five years, large companies have scrambled to develop digital transformation programmes. These are multi-million-pound projects to overhaul antiquated IT systems and technology infrastructure.

Freelancers can undergo their own digital transformation for a fraction of the cost and likely reap even greater rewards. When you break it down, a digital transformation is simply a commitment to using technology in the best way possible to make your working life easier and more efficient. In practice this means:

- Going digital: Taking your business online is one of the most effective strategies for growth. If your core business requires you to be physically present then consider taking parts of it online. If you're a nail artist, can you offer online courses alongside your manicures? If you can't take your services online (you can't actually do nails virtually) can you at least take your bookings online, so you don't waste time scheduling them in?
- Documenting your processes: When you come to hire help or team members, you'll need an easy way to

show them how to do things. If you document how
you do your work, getting someone to replicate it will
be seamless.

- Automating what you can: Related to the point
  above, automate as much as possible. I'm very happy
  to hand over my admin to the robots because it
  means I can spend more time working on the areas
  of my business that only I can do. Automation means
  scheduling services, auto-reminders on payments,
  auto-bills, etc.

Structural efficiency

Most freelancer businesses are relatively straightforward but
it's still likely that, over the years, your business will change.
It might evolve organically into a slightly different offering
or you might intentionally pivot what you do to a totally
different area. Either way, it's important to regularly assess
whether the structure of your business still makes sense.
Make a habit of doing this when you do your tax return
each year – you're looking at your profits anyway so it's the
perfect time.

- Your legal set-up: As I covered in the first chapter
  of this book, you have different options for setting
  up your business with the tax and legal authorities.
  After you've been freelancing for some time, it's worth
  reassessing whether that structure still works for you.
  Seek advice from an accountant or an independent
  financial advisor about whether it's time to change that
  set-up.

- Scalable income: Is all of your work dependent on you exchanging your time for money? Are there ways for you to scale some aspects of your business so that you can increase your profits without having to work more hours?
- Automation: Scalable income streams also allow you to introduce processes into your workflow, enabling you to bring on additional support so that you don't have to be constantly present in your business for it to keep running.
- Revenue streams: How many revenue streams do you have and are they all still working for you? Not having enough revenue streams leaves you open to risk should you lose that work but having too many can spread you too thin. Keep tabs on how much money your different revenue streams are generating for you and also how much time you're spending on them.

Financial efficiency

If your personal budget is looking tight, what do you do? You cut your expenditure. When you're thinking about efficiency, however, it's not quite as black and white. The truism 'spend more to make more' holds water, although I tweak the saying to 'spend smarter, earn faster'. You're not looking to cut out your subscriptions, you're looking at where you get the most return on your investment. Are you investing in your skills through personal and professional development? What subscriptions and services benefit you and your business and which ones are sucking up resources? Is it time for a gear upgrade?

The Six Basics of Growing a Business

Growth comes in different shapes and sizes. It doesn't mean going from a freelancer who works alone to running a 1,000-strong team overnight. There are, however, some core principles when it comes to scaling a business. Here are the six basics of growing any business, which you can use as a foundation for thinking about what growth can look like for you.

1. Increase sales

When you think about growing your business, your first idea will probably be to increase what you're selling. That strategy is indeed a great place to start. Increasing sales simply means selling more things. This can be done by attracting new customers or clients, selling more to your existing ones, or a combination of both. You do this by working on your marketing strategy in order to target new customers as well as to communicate to your existing ones what other products or services you have to offer.

Increasing your sales also means looking at your prices. In *Pricing for Profit*, chartered accountant Peter Hill says that the most impactful way to grow a business is to increase your prices. 'The quickest and greatest impact on profits comes from simply charging a little more on the price,' he says. As you grow your business, don't neglect the simple act of raising your prices on an annual basis.

2. Improve what you sell

No matter how long you've been in business, there's always room to improve your offering. If you want to improve what you're selling – whether it's an online course, a haircut or handmade jewellery – start by asking for feedback from the people who are already buying from you. If you sell directly to customers, a survey is a simple and effective way to do this. You can use services like Typeform, SurveyMonkey or Google Forms to create a survey that you can share with your customers. Keep it short and sweet so that people are more likely to fill it out. There are only a handful of questions that you really need the answer to:

- What do you buy from me and why?
- What do you value most about my products/services?
- What could I do to make my product/service more valuable to you?
- What would encourage you to buy more from me?

If you work with clients, you can still get feedback. Either ask them for a ten-minute call or send them a short email at the end of your projects. Ask them questions like:

- Why do you like working with me?
- What could I do to improve how we work together?
- What would make you hire me again?

Not only will the positive feedback from customers and clients make you feel great, it's also a valuable source of information you can use to bolster your business.

3. Make new things to sell

You might have saturated your existing market with your current products or services or you might fancy a new challenge. Either way, making new things to sell is a great way to grow any business.

Just like improving your existing offering, when you develop new products or services, you'll want to start with your existing customer base. Talk to your existing clients and customers to find out what new products or services they'd want from you. Then, test those new ideas out with them. As you're developing your ideas, also conduct market research to understand the potential wider audience.

4. Hire a team

Growth also comes in the form of physically expanding the size of your team. For many freelancers, the thought of hiring a team can be a daunting prospect because you're so used to working alone. But it doesn't have to mean taking on full-time staff; a freelance virtual assistant or bookkeeper doing a few of hours of work a month can transform your business.

Make a list of all your time-consuming clerical tasks. These might include diary management, social media posting, checking email, keeping track of expenses and answering customer queries. Once you see it all written down, you'll realise how much you're in need of help. Rather than try to find one person who can take care of it all, start with the most pressing task and find someone to do that. You can always expand the scope later down the line or hire an additional freelancer to take care of a different responsibility. If you're worried about allowing someone else to check your emails or take care of your finances, find someone you can trust by asking for recommendations from your freelance network. And always remember to have them sign a contract.

5. Find new sources of funding

If you feel like you've hit the ceiling of how much money you can make doing what you currently do, but need more capital to grow your business, it's time to start looking for new sources of funding. This can come in the form of loans, selling shares to outside investors or grants. You can also invest any profits you've made back into your business. Go back to chapter five if you need a refresher on developing additional revenue streams and external funding options.

6. Bring in an outside perspective

Most freelance businesses get to a stage where they need an outsider's perspective to propel them forward. You can do this in a number of ways, depending on where you're at with your business, as well as your budget.

Mentorship is typically free and offers a way to gain insights and advice from someone more experienced or further along in their career than you. Mentorship is especially useful if you don't have formal training or a large professional network to lean on.

You can also hire a business coach who can help you overcome specific obstacles. Coaches typically focus on mindset issues, helping you see things from a different angle, and will give you exercises to change how you're going about things. This option might be right for you if you want to focus on developing your soft skills.

If your issue is technical, you might consider hiring a financial advisor or business consultant. For example, if you're struggling with the fundamentals of your business model or are trying to decide whether it's time to change the structure of your business, an independent financial advisor can assist you.

There's a list of business support services in the directory on page 303 which include sites where you can find mentors and coaches.

What Do You Believe About Work?

I have three core beliefs about work – it should be fun, simple and meaningful. That's not, however, to say I think work should be easy.

When I say work should be simple, I mean that it doesn't need to be overly complicated. If you're a freelance writer, the main function of your job should be writing. You don't need to get bogged down doing projects you don't enjoy but have read somewhere will make you rich or happy.

By the same token, when I say work should be meaningful, it needs to be meaningful to *you*. Lifestyle blogging and taking photographs of makeup might not spark you up but it sure does for some people. Equally, not everyone will find their purpose in admirable work like healthcare. I would make a terrible doctor but I find a lot of meaning in helping people build working lives that suit them.

I really do believe work can be fun. I grew up at a time when pop culture told us work was boring. *The Office*, *The Simpsons* and *Peep Show* had us believe that work meant dreary commutes, bad coffee and shuffling papers around a desk until it was time to clock off. Then I went to journalism school and, on my first day, one of my professors told the class, 'This is going to be fun.' His motto was that journalism was supposed to be enjoyable. I ran with that lesson – the idea that our jobs could be fun turned my working world upside down. I still hold a tight grasp on those beliefs about work. I like to regularly ask myself: 'Am I living those beliefs on a daily basis, through the projects I'm doing?'

Sometimes work that once fulfilled us no longer does and it's OK to let that go. Just like we grow apart from people in our lives, we also grow apart from our work. One of the reasons I love being a journalist is because it has a get-out-of-jail-free card built in. At any point, it's totally fine to switch the area you write about and move on to a new story. Over the course of my journalism career, I've written about everything from local government and education policy to electronic music and nightlife culture. At the time, I loved writing about those topics. They were fun and I found meaning in them. But then I outgrew them. My interests changed and led me to new areas of work. In my bid to always keep things simple, I let those old interests go. It wasn't easy and, just like growing apart from a friend or partner stings, so does saying goodbye to work that once filled you up. But from that space, new life grows.

Chapter Summary: In It for the Long Haul

Whether you're ready to take your freelancing to the next level or thinking about a new job, give yourself permission to do what's right for you and your career.

Know when to quit: Tools like the Quitting Quadrant can help you learn how to let go of projects or work that's no longer serving you.

Don't wait for a boss to promote you: It's your business, so recognise the value of your own work by giving yourself better perks, hiring an assistant or creating a bonus system for yourself.

Work less, do more: Work on streamlining all aspects of your business. This will not only maximise your profits but also give you back more time.

The six basics of growing a business: If you're ready to grow, explore how you can: increase sales; improve what you sell; make new things to sell; hire a team; find new sources of funding; or bring in an outside perspective.

The Self in Self-employment

When I was in primary school, I made a magazine with my classmate after school. Much to our parents' chagrin, we printed out dozens of colour copies on our home printers, stapled them together and posted them through the neighbours' letterboxes. The economics of that venture didn't really add up but we were eight years old and didn't understand the extortionate cost of printer ink.

Ten years later, while at university, I had another go at making magazines when I produced my own gig listings guide. I must have learned something from my previous attempt because this time round, I persuaded local businesses to take out adverts to cover the printing costs. When I graduated, I closed the business with £200 in profit. Nothing to set the business world alight with but a big boost to a new graduate's summer plans.

Back then, I thought those forays into magazine publishing were a sign that I was supposed to work in the media industry. So when I first entered the workforce by landing an editorial assistant job at a magazine, I couldn't understand why I was so disappointed. I thought it must just be that the company wasn't 'prestigious' enough. So after 18 months, off I went to find a new job at a national broadsheet newspaper. I ticked the prestige box but this time I was really bored by the focus of the job. Next came a master's degree in journalism. And so, this was how my first decade of employment played out: I was a career goldilocks, perpetually dissatisfied and undervalued, clawing my way up the career ladder, until eventually it was pulled out from underneath me.

I lost my job and started working for myself. Self-employment came about by accident but, looking back now, all the signs had not, as I thought, pointed towards magazine publishing but to me building a creative, entrepreneurial career for myself. I don't regret taking the path I did to get here because I wouldn't have known how to listen to those early signals anyway. I grew up in an age and culture that didn't champion self-employment or value entrepreneurialism. Now that I know what's possible when you strike out alone, there's no looking back for me.

The single biggest surprise about self-employment has been just how much it really is about the *self*. I've learned a heck of a lot about how to run a business since I struck out on my own but I've learned even more about who *I* am. At a surface level, it's not surprising that I've been able to spend more time on self-development because the simple truth is I have more time to devote to it. The two hours each day I'd spend commuting to and from work are now *my* time, allowing me to sleep better, exercise more and generally commit to myself. But there's more to it than that. Being a business of one means if I'm not operating at my best, nor is my business. This doesn't mean I need to hack my life to maximise my efficiency, though. It's about creating a symbiotic relationship between my work and my life. One in which I can work in a way that works for me and allows me to perform at my best because I've put my personal needs first.

It's no accident that no two days are quite the same in this career that I've designed for myself. I used to beat myself up for getting bored at work, not understanding why I couldn't focus and sit still at my desk in the same way my colleagues seemed able to. It turns out that I need variety to thrive. Learning that has meant I now know how important it is for me to regularly shake things up. That can be as simple as switching up my workspace or as challenging as starting a new project from scratch. Similarly, I used to think procrastination was about laziness and that there was something wrong with me whenever I delayed a task. When I found out that actually it's to do with discharging uncomfortable emotions, a weight was lifted off my shoulders. I wasn't lazy for struggling to meet the deadline for this book, I was just riddled with self-doubt. Since learning this, I've given myself more of a break. I can't say I've kicked the habit of procrastinating but at least I've cultivated a greater sense of understanding about *why* I do it.

Who knew that curiosity could be such a valuable trait in business? For me it's fuelled some of my most success-ful ventures. It was curiosity that led me to try something bold and charge a subscription fee for my newsletter. Could I turn content people usually expect to receive for free into a sustainable media business? Turns out, I could. When I gave myself permission to see new projects as experiments, trying something new just out of sheer interest in what might happen didn't feel so daunting. Meanwhile, it was a frus-trated kind of curiosity that led me to start campaigning for freelance workers' rights. I was driven by simply wondering if it was possible for things to be better than the status quo.

I once dreaded speaking in public and navigating small talk at networking events. I put this down to me being an introvert. Working in a way that preserves my energy has made me realise that when given the chance to keep my batteries full, I *can* go out and do high-energy activities when I need and want to. Not only that but I actually like it. The world is designed with extroverts in mind but that doesn't mean introverts can't thrive in it as well. I learned that when I respect what my body is trying to tell me, everything in my life – including my work – is better for it.

For me, who I work with is as important as the work itself. I thought freelancing would be a lonely business but it's been the opposite – my friends are my colleagues and my colleagues are my friends. I've made friends through a vibrant network of ambitious people who just 'get' it. I've launched creative projects with friends and pinched myself that I've been able to call that work.

It's been one of the most difficult but illuminating realisations to accept that progress isn't linear. In traditional employment, I couldn't see a path for myself and I believed that success meant prestige. I was ambitious and keen to progress but I wasn't interested in a management role so eventually I hit a ceiling in terms of my growth prospects. And even though working for a big company made me think I was important, the actual work left me feeling empty. Now, nothing lights me up more than being able to see my work make a tangible difference to someone's life. Freelancing offered me the chance to stitch myself a job that challenged me but didn't divert me from my purpose. I have, however, needed to make peace with just how winding the road is. And so I've rewritten my definition of success. Now I consider myself successful if I'm able to work – and therefore, live – on my own terms.

I've also learned how to let my less desirable character traits exist harmoniously within my business. I'm impatient, which means when I decide to do something, I want to take action on it right away. This has been great for launching business ideas and starting projects but has made the waiting process impossible to bear at times. And when I think about why I'm so passionate about fighting for freelancers' rights, it comes down to an almost childlike feeling of indignation. I just hate feeling like I'm second rate. Why should freelancers suffer injustices? Why can't we get paid on time? Shouldn't everyone, regardless of their employment status, be able to take time off to have a kid? When I first stuck my head above the parapet and started campaigning for freelancers' rights, the thought crossed my mind that it might jeopardise my career. I'd seen power imbalances in the workplace too, however I was too scared of losing my job to do anything about them. But once I was on my own, the exhaustion of feeling like the little guy at the mercy of the powers that be took over. I've always had a tendency for righteous outrage but now I've finally found a healthy outlet for it.

How do you secure your future in an uncertain world? By staying curious, leaning into your personality traits and just enjoying the ride. All you can do is learn to focus on the process and let go of the outcome. I used to think that business skills were all about learning how to be a hard-nosed negotiator or a slick salesperson and getting so good at Excel that you don't need a mouse. It's been transformative to realise that my existing skills, especially the softer ones, have played such a vital role in building my business. In fact, I've been able to create a career that works for me because I've focused on my strengths but also leaned into my weaknesses. You too already have all the skills you need to build a thriving career on your own. Sure, there'll be some bumps along the way but there's nothing more fulfilling than taking control of your career and building the life that you've always wanted. Work on yourself as much as you do your business. After all, you are the business.

Directory

Freelance marketplaces and jobs boards
Hoxby: hoxby.com
Contently: contently.com
Yuno Juno: www.yunojuno.com
Worksome: worksome.co.uk
Freelancer Club: freelancerclub.net
The Dots: the-dots.com

Unions and trade bodies
National Union of Journalists: www.nuj.org.uk
Equity: www.equity.org.uk
Association for Independent Professionals and the Self-Employed: www.ipse.co.uk
Bectu Union: bectu.org.uk

Government pages on self-employment and tax
www.gov.uk/set-up-self-employed
www.gov.uk/topic/business-tax/self-employed

Regulations
Late Payment of Commercial Debts regulations: www.gov.uk/late-commercial-payments-interest-debt-recovery
Maternity Allowance: www.gov.uk/maternity-allowance

Health and Safety: www.hse.gov.uk/self-employed
Anti-discrimination: www.gov.uk/guidance/equality-act-2010-guidance
Advertising Standards: asa.org.uk

Accounting and bookkeeping software
Xero: www.xero.com/uk
Sage: www.sage.com/en-gb/sage-business-cloud/accounting
FreeAgent: www.freeagent.com
Quickbooks: quickbooks.intuit.com/uk
Crunch: www.crunch.co.uk
Clear Books: www.clearbooks.co.uk

Office furniture suppliers
Wellworking: www.wellworking.co.uk
Andrews Office Furniture: www.andrewsofficefurniture.com

Digital nomad trips
Hacker Paradise: www.hackerparadise.org
Remote Year: remoteyear.com

Co-working spaces
WeWork: www.wework.com
Fora: www.foraspace.com
Third Door: www.third-door.com
Second Home: secondhome.io

Digital communities
Leapers (for all freelancers, free): leapers.co
Freelance Heroes (for all freelancers, free): facebook.com/groups/freelanceheroes

r/freelance (for all freelancers, free): reddit.com/r/freelance
The Freelance Lifestylers (for all freelancers, free): facebook.com/groups/freelancelifestyle
Doing It for The Kids (for freelance parents, free): www.facebook.com/groups/DIFTK
Writers Hour (for writers and authors, free and paid): writershour.com
Society of Freelance Journalists (for journalists and writers, free): freelancesoc.org
No1 Freelance Media Women (for female media freelancers, free): facebook.com/groups/No1FreelanceMediaWomen
The Coven Girl Gang (for female freelancers, paid): thecovengirlgang.com

Business support services
Mentorship schemes: www.mentorsme.co.uk
Free and independent financial advice for businesses: thebusinessfinanceguide.co.uk

Government page with finance and support for businesses
www.gov.uk/business-finance-support

Advice lines
Citizens Advice: citizensadvice.org.uk or 0800 144 8848 (England) 0800 702 2020 (Wales)
HMRC: gov.uk/contact-hmrc or 0300 200 3310 (tax helpline)
Maternity Action: maternityaction.org.uk/get-free-advice
Money Advice Service: moneyadviceservice.org.uk or 0800 138 7777
Small Business Commissioner (for help with late payments): smallbusinesscommissioner.gov.uk or 0121 695 7770

Books

Real Life Money: An honest guide to taking control of your finances, Clare Seal

Never Split the Difference: Negotiating as if your life depended on it, Chris Voss with Tahl Raz

Pricing for Profit: How to develop a powerful pricing strategy for your business, Peter Hill

The Multi-Hyphen Method: Work less, create more: how to make your side hustle work for you, Emma Gannon

Start with Why: How great leaders inspire everyone to take action, Simon Sinek

Open up: The power of talking about money, Alex Holder

The Millionaire Next Door: The surprising secrets of America's wealthy, Thomas J. Stanley

Profit First: Transform your business from a cash-eating monster to a money-making machine, Mike Michalowicz

Company of One: Why staying small is the next big thing for business, Paul Jarvis

You're Not Broke, You're Pre-Rich: How to streamline your finances, stay in control of your bank balance and have more £££, Emilie Bellet

Money: A User's Guide, Laura Whateley

The Four Tendencies: The indispensable personality profiles that reveal how to make your life better (and other people's lives better, too), Gretchen Rubin

The Big Leap: Conquer your hidden fear and take life to the next level, Gay Hendricks

Deep Work: Rules for focused success in a distracted world, Cal Newport

Believe, Build, Become: How to supercharge your career, Anna Jones and Debbie Wosskow

Acknowledgements

I might work for myself, but I didn't write this book alone.

Firstly, a huge thanks to my literary agent, Lucy Morris, for looking after me and for being the best teammate I could ask for. And to the rest of the Curtis Brown team, with special thanks to Vanessa Fogarty. The team at Ebury Edge who brought this book to life. Lucy Oates – thank you for understanding this book, and me, from our very first Zoom meeting and for making my first book writing experience an utter joy. And to Liz Marvin, whose meticulous edits made this book better.

I wouldn't be writing this book at all were it not for my newsletter readers, the worldwide LANCE family. What started as a project to regain some semblance of creativity after losing my job turned into a life-changing decision. And a special thanks to the freelancers who help me produce the newsletter, Eléonore Hamelin for illustrating it each week and Ebony-Storm Halliday for looking after it while I took time off to write this book. And the team at Substack for believing in the power of independent writing, especially Hamish McKenzie for encouraging me to take the leap and turn my newsletter into a viable business.

To my army of work wives, thank you for the endless supply of support, cheerleading and encouragement. Tiffany

Philippou, my best friend and now colleague, I could fill a book just with thanks for all that you do for me – from introducing me to my agent, to sending me daily pep talks via voice note – my never-ending gratitude to you. Claudia Wallace, Sian Meades-Williams, Harriet Minter, Megha Mohan, The Pea Latte Lads and the FU PAY ME gang, I would be lost without your career counsel. A special thank you to the London Writers Salon, without your 8am writers' hours, this book wouldn't have been written. And to my fellow freelance campaigners and activists, who work tirelessly to make our industry a better place: Martin Lewis. Matthew Knight. Matt Dowling. Tatiana Morris-Walk. Jen A Miller. Wudan Yan. Ellie Phillips. Alex Holder. Emilie Bellet. Alice Tapper.

Thank you to the people who gave me a chance early on. Michael Shapiro for teaching me that writing doesn't have to be painful and that journalism can, in fact, be a lot of fun. Emily Bell for teaching me to embrace digital media but still be critical of it. Vicky Spratt for landing me my first freelance paycheque. Matthew Anderson for commissioning me to write for my dream publication. Dolly Alderton and Pandora Sykes for giving me a regular fact-checking gig. Rowena Cumners for championing my podcast. Meghan Musante and Jesse Steinbach and the rest of the Dell team for being my most reliable clients in the midst of a global pandemic. And to my friend and accountant, Mike Psaras, for making sure all my tax figures are present and correct. These milestones all gave me the confidence to keep going in my DIY career.

To my family. Mum, for teaching me that financial independence is a feminist issue and that you can achieve anything with the right spreadsheet. Dad, for always being proud of me and for encouraging all my dreams, no matter how weird. Taia, you also just published your first book (at age 92!) and, as ever, showed me how wildly fulfilling a creative career can be. Thank you. Thank you. Thank you. And finally, to Chris, for washing up my endless stream of mugs (after making me endless cups of tea), for walking the dogs when I was on deadline and for believing that I can do whatever I sent my mind to, your love and support was the fuel that kept me going. My solo career is anything but lonely with you around.

Index